Afterschool Education:
Approaches to an Emerging Field

Afterschool Education: Approaches to an Emerging Field

Gil G. Noam

Gina Biancarosa

Nadine Dechausay

Harvard Education Press

Library of Congress Control Number 2002112415
ISBN 1-891792-07-5

Published by Harvard Education Press,
an imprint of the Harvard Education Publishing Group

Harvard Education Press
8 Story Street, 5th Floor
Cambridge, MA 02138

Cover Design: Kate Canfield
Editorial Production: Dody Riggs
Typography: Sheila Walsh

The typeface used in the book is Giovanni Book.

Contents

Preface

The recent surge of interest in afterschool programs, along with a dramatic increase in funding, offers educators a unique and exciting opportunity to strengthen learning beyond the school day. Afterschool programming offers one contemporary means of bringing to life the ideas of great school reformers and educational theorists such as John Dewey, Rudolf Steiner, Howard Gardner, and Ted Sizer, all of whom stress the importance of deep, experiential, and participatory learning to a growing mind and society. Afterschool programs offer the ideal conditions for this kind of learning with their small groups, voluntary participation, lack of bureaucracy, chances to experiment continually with new content and materials, and opportunities to forge strong relationships among peers, as well as between staff and students.

However, in order to realize their immense potential, afterschool programs will require a great deal of theoretical and practical support. Our motivation for researching the existing knowledge and practices in afterschool settings was to help "scaffold" the field's development by creating typologies that will help practitioners, researchers, and policymakers in the field evolve a clear and coherent plan of action.

This book represents the culmination of over a year of intense work. It began as a white paper that served as the foundation for the conference entitled Afterschool Settings: Learning with Excitement, which was held in February 2002 at the Harvard Graduate School of Education (HGSE) and sponsored by Harvard's Program in Afterschool Education and Research (PAER) in collaboration with McLean Hospital's Developmental Psychology Research Program.[1] The paper and conference served as PAER's first step in an ambitious agenda of future research, technical assistance, city-

---

1. For additional information on the organizations mentioned in this preface, please see Appendix A.

wide initiatives, and training to be developed collaboratively with national and local experts, afterschool practitioners, foundations, and Harvard's host communities (the Allston-Brighton, Fenway, and Mission Hill sections of Boston, and Cambridge, Massachusetts).

The paper and conference were made possible by a grant from Robert Kargman and a five-year commitment by Harvard to strengthen afterschool learning environments in Boston. Kargman, a Boston-based businessman with strong ties to HGSE, approached the senior author with the idea of creating an annual conference to address promising practices and strategies that promote quality afterschool programming. We decided on a first conference that would bring practitioners, funders, policymakers, and researchers from Cambridge, Boston, and across the country to Harvard to discuss and debate the development of afterschool education as a field. Our paper would produce an in-depth review and provide recommendations in the area of learning in afterschool settings; together they would serve as the starting point and focus for the conference. We began inviting panelists for the conference and were surprised by the overwhelmingly enthusiastic response. Clearly, we had hit a nerve. The Nellie Mae Education Foundation generously provided additional funding to bring speakers and participants to Cambridge from across the country.

By this time we had completed the white paper. Our scope was both local and national: we interviewed national leaders and talked to participants in the afterschool movement at many levels of expertise; we also focused a great number of our inquiries on Harvard's local host communities. One year earlier, Harvard University had made a historic commitment to create a better infrastructure for afterschool programs. Five million dollars for five years were committed and the Harvard After-School Initiative (HASI) became a founding member of the largest Boston private-public collaboration serving children and families: the Afterschool for All Partnership. Under the mayor's leadership and chaired by successful entrepreneur Chris Gabrieli, thirteen foundations, corporations, businesses, and organizations committed more than $23 million to expand available slots in programs, to work toward sustainability, and to improve quality by focusing on learning.

Harvard is the only institution of higher education in the Partnership and does not see its role as solely to provide funds. We are attempting to create interest in afterschool throughout the university, to build bridges to the community, and to train our undergraduate and graduate students in collaboration with community organizations. We are also developing courses that deal with afterschool education, which will generate additional interest among undergraduate and graduate students to volunteer in programs throughout the city.

PAER addressed the goal of improving afterschool programs through learning when it took on the report and conference that evolved into this book. We have made many changes since we were invited by the Harvard Education Press to create the book, including the incorporation of many conference participants' suggestions and criticisms, and the addition of a number of commentaries by our panelists.

It is exciting to have such strong partners in our efforts to increase visibility and academic rigor in this growing field. We have already mentioned our funders, Robert Kargman, Nellie Mae, and HASI, but we wish to formally thank them here for their continued support and encouragement of our efforts. Robert continues to be a friend and someone who has a deep appreciation of the significance of community-building and afterschool education. Nellie Mae is led by a wise and forceful president, Blenda Wilson. She and her program officers Gene Lee and Lynn D'Ambrose are dedicated to many of the topics raised in this book. For their contributions to our thoughts and the field in general, we also wish to thank our colleagues on the HASI executive committee—Jane Corlette, Kevin McCluskey, Paige Lewin, Judith Kidd, and Judy Palfrey—and the consultants—Andrew Bundy and Elaine Fersh. We thank Ronay and Richard Menschel, Paul Sidel, and Bill Thompson for all they do to support our work. We are also very grateful to Dean Joel Monell at HGSE, to our new Dean Ellen Condliffe Lagemann, and to Bruce Cohen, president of McLean Hospital, for their strong support of our work.

Additionally, we wish to thank all those who attended the February 2002 conference for their thoughtful and enthusiastic participation, which helped shape our revisions and expansions. We particularly appreciate the contributions of the panelists and discussants who prepared formal responses to the conference white paper: Tina Blythe, An Me Chung, Jennifer Davis, Mary Lou Fishman, Lucy Friedman, Chris Gabrieli, Tim Garvin,

Carrie Hickey, Inez Johnson, Leigh Van Dyken, Laura Wolhafe, and Bernie Zubrowski. We further want to express our gratitude to conference panelists Harris Cooper, Adriana de Kanter, Reed Larson, Pilar O'Cadiz, Sam Piha, and Marcelo Suárez-Orozco, who revised transcripts of their commentaries for inclusion in this volume despite an extremely tight schedule. In completing our reviews of the literature for each chapter, we owe much to our committed research assistants and associates, Jennifer Boyd, Sara Heller, Elena Reilly, Jodi Rosenbaum, and Lisa Wahl. Further thanks are due our colleagues at PAER for their comments, support, and inspiring work in the field. We also owe a debt of gratitude to our professional writer and editor, Andrew L. Wilson, who helped meld our writing styles and offered critical feedback. Doug Clayton and his team at the Harvard Education Publishing Group are also due our thanks for their patience and editorial advice. Finally, our thanks would not be complete if we did not thank Patricia Quintin and Pat Furia, administrative assistants at PAER and McLean. And, as always, many thanks for insight, inspiration, and support to Maryanne Wolf, Ben, and David!

We hope this volume captivates and inspires your thinking about afterschool education, and that it will further all subsequent efforts to create a viable and sustainable field of practice and scholarship.

Gil G. Noam
Gina Biancarosa
Nadine Dechausay

Introduction

These are exciting times for the field of afterschool education. Working in this emerging field, we have a chance to define, refine, and transform the learning opportunities of millions of children and youth. It has been estimated that young people in this country spend almost a third of their organized time (including school hours) in afterschool and summer programs, and there is a growing recognition that such programs should be used to strengthen learning. The field is bursting with creative ideas, and so many promising models and trials are now underway that it would be impossible to catalog them all.

Yet the challenging work of creating a system of learning—incorporating a trained staff, readily available curricula, and an array of well-researched model practices—has barely begun, and there exists little systematic and conclusive research on afterschool to guide our practices. Therefore, in this book, we have attempted to define the field of afterschool learning in such a way as to make sense of the major topics that emerged in our interviews and observations of existing programs, discussions with program leaders, and our own demonstration projects. We chose to focus our efforts on three essential aspects of afterschool learning—bridging school to afterschool; homework, or extended learning; and curricula, or enriched learning—leaving other equally crucial topics (e.g., tutor-training and supervision, the use of new technology, the development of age-appropriate learning strategies, and finding the best ways to connect afterschool to the community) for future consideration. We intend to refine and develop the ideas expressed in this book and to sharpen our collaboration with schools, afterschool programs, and community organizations. Our goal is to make this research and development effort relevant and immediately applicable to the current learning conditions of children and youth.

The afterschool movement consists of different constituencies that share general goals yet diverge greatly on strategies. The growing number of policymakers, researchers, service providers, teachers, parents, and youth making up the field of afterschool education today do not speak with a unified voice on all subjects. The greatest current philosophical divide in the afterschool movement is that which exists between representatives of community youth development organizations and schools. In general, school reformers, superintendents, principals, and teachers tend to emphasize the goal of academic alignment, while youth development advocates and staff of community organizations tend to focus their energies on fostering democratic participation in group learning activities, nurturing physical skills through sports, and relaxed play. These orientations frequently clash, and thus have to be recognized and addressed in any learning initiative.

Recently, due to changed funding streams (e.g., 21st Century Community Learning Centers) and an increased recognition that institutions must jointly serve children and families in order to solve the complex challenges of education, there has been considerable progress in overcoming this school-versus-community-program divide.[1] The new collaborative spirit has great implications for setting learning goals, because it brings with it potential information, communication, and even alignment across learning environments. But it also raises significant dangers. For example, the call for "alignment of learning" in afterschool could become synonymous with the demand for an extended school day: a significant danger according to many in the field (Halpern, 1999; S. Richards Scott, personal communication, July 17, 2001). Conversely, school administrators might be tempted to cut arts, sports, and projects during the school day in order to concentrate on academic test preparation, relegating these crucial activities to the afterschool hours. Because not all children participate in afterschool activities, such a policy would amount to depriving many children of significant non-academic skill and talent building during school hours.

---

1. In the last five years, funding for 21st Century Community Learning Centers has increased exponentially from $1 million in 1997 to $1 billion in 2002. Until the most recent renewal of this legislation, programs had to initiate collaborations between schools and community-based organizations to be eligible for this funding. Presently an increase to $1.5 billion is under consideration in Congress.

Despite many differences in focus, it is possible to identify a growing consensus regarding afterschool programming articulated around the following points:

- The afterschool hours should be structured differently from the school day, in order to provide a varied experience for children and youth.
- Fun, mentoring, and enrichment should form some part of these hours.
- Programs should support the academic learning of the school day by supporting basic skills and homework, as well as by providing tutoring for academically at-risk children.
- Programs should experiment with other forms of learning, such as projects, service learning, and outdoors adventures to deepen school learning and create new interests and abilities.
- Programs should encourage the widest and richest connections possible with the community and with families, and they should make an effort to expose children to the different cultures found in their communities.[2]
- Programs should encourage children to pursue their own learning and to set goals for themselves.

While content in afterschool differs greatly, the way in which time is structured proved surprisingly consistent across the afterschool programs we surveyed. In general, afterschool programs consist of three main blocks:

1. homework help and tutoring
2. projects, service-learning, journalism, and other enriched learning experiences that are not directly tied to the school days
3. non-academic activities such as sports, crafts, and play

Obviously, each of these three aspects of programming possesses a learning component. Yet each has different goals, involves a different relationship to school learning, and demands a different skill set from providers.

2. This was described by Sam Piha (personal communication, January 10, 2002).

Extended Learning

Homework help and tutoring is a direct extension of the school day, typically defined and checked by teachers. As homework tutors, afterschool staff inevitably serves as an extension of the school day staff. We therefore refer to homework and related learning in afterschool programs as extended learning. Extended learning is "aligned" to the learning that occurs during the school day.

Enriched Learning

Project-based learning activities embody a philosophy of learning distinct from the merely academic, emphasizing self-direction, exploration, and hands-on experience. Such activities can either be highly aligned to academic, school-based learning, or function in an unconnected manner. Some programs, for example, take science or social studies curricula from the school day and develop museum trips, community service, or apprenticeships around these school goals. Other programs develop projects with their students that are entirely focused on the afterschool world, with no tie back to academic curricula. Given the participatory nature of choosing projects, in many programs the link between project-based and school learning can be no more than accidental. But the actual intentional goals of projects produce many transferable skills, from intention and motivation to flexibility, understanding, and research strategies. These projects can enhance learning preparedness and school attachment, which are widely recognized as two essential ingredients to academic success. Because of the potential of this type of learning for enriching children's experiences of education, we refer to it as enriched learning.

Intentional Learning and Programming

These activities foster non-academic skills and social abilities in young people. Such activities not only provide a balance to the day's programming for all children, but also are especially important for those who have chronically bad experiences during the school day. This type of programming is mostly not directly aligned with school, although it takes place in programs with or without other connections to the school day. Such learning activities are commonly referred to in youth development circles as "intentional programming." We therefore refer to the kind of learning that occurs during intentional programming as intentional learning. Of course, most learning is intentional, in that it involves some intention on the part of the teacher and/or learner. In this sense, extended and enriched learning are also intentional. However, we use the phrase "intentional learning" in this book to describe a type of learning that does not depend upon standard academic or special curricula—a type of learning that results from programming efforts to promote learning in social, emotional, and extracurricular ways. In other words, we wish to emphasize that non-academic activities do in fact promote learning.

Our research leads us to conclude that afterschool time can be most effective and rewarding for children when programs achieve a balance between these three types of learning.

Afterschool Programs as Intermediary Spaces

As intermediary spaces, produced by vibrant collaborations between different institutions and forces such as schools, families, community-based organizations, cultural institutions, and university programs, afterschool programs can work as intermediary environments (Noam, 2001), giving children a safe platform for exploration of the various forms of learning and helping them to situate their learning in the wider context of their communities. We describe afterschools as intermediary for several reasons: they do not belong to any one group or organization, and in order to function they require the coordination of various stakeholders and "part owners" using flexible methods of management and conflict resolution. Afterschool connects to academic work without serving as a school, takes on aspects of family life (such as comfort, security, recreation) without becoming a family, and instills community-consciousness in children without becoming a civic group. Such flexibility creates risks, such as the risk of power struggles between competing groups and interests, but it is also a source of extremely productive tension and a stimulus to creativity, leadership, and effective time use. We believe that afterschool programs should define themselves not by the criteria of efficiency, but by the richness of the learning they foster and the depth of the connections they enable between different worlds. These goals require partnership at all levels. As is the pattern in all social reform movements, our current great expectations of afterschool programming will inevitably be tempered by growing realism. However, we can still seize this unique moment by focusing our anticipation, attention, and energy to create ever-improving conditions for expanding children's learning opportunities during afterschool hours.

Methods

Our core research and writing team was assembled in June of 2001 at the Program in Afterschool Education and Research (PAER) at the Harvard Graduate School of Education (see Appendix A for a description of PAER and related initiatives). Over the course of a year, the team culled information on the core topics of this report from a variety of sources. Interviews served as a major source of information. Specifically, we conducted interviews with a sample of practitioners and leaders, representing the wide variety of roles and theoretical perspectives in the afterschool field today. We made a strenuous effort to interview each of the programs in host communities (Allston-Brighton, Fenway, Mission Hill, and Cambridge) with the goal of getting direct input from programs that we hope to support through technical assistance (see Appendix B for a map and descriptions of these communities). We felt it crucial not to stop at transmitting our idea of promising practices, but to elicit input on what is most important and useful to educators working in the field.

Overall, we were encouraged by the enthusiasm with which our requests for interviews were received and the openness in sharing experiences and views demonstrated by both practitioners and leaders (see Appendix C for a list of those interviewed). For the purpose of these interviews, we developed a survey and a semistructured interview protocol. Although we make sparing use of actual quotations drawn from interviews, our report is informed throughout by their content, as well as by the PAER conference "Afterschool Settings: Learning with Excitement" held in February 2002 at HGSE. The participants at this conference contributed greatly to our revisions, and indeed a number of panelists from the conference revised their own comments for inclusion in this volume. Finally, our own experiences with the Harvard After-school Initiative, Responsive Advocacy for Life and Learning in Youth (RALLY), Gaining Early Awareness and Readiness for Undergraduate Programs (GEAR UP), Project Zero, the Mental Health Initiative of McLean Hospital, PAER, and other Harvard-affiliated programs and projects also informed our thinking.

Our data collection effort was not intended to render a complete picture of all aspects of afterschool learning, but rather to serve as an empirical base for refining and extending debate on this topic and to create a plan of action for our work in the next five years. In the course of our research, we drew upon the following types of data sources:

- interviews and discussions with leaders in the field
- interviews with program directors
- existing research studies
- policy briefs and theoretical papers
- observations in programs
- volunteer questionnaires
- experiences in our own demonstration sites and consulting and evaluation experience in New York City, Boston, Cambridge, Denver, and California

By combining these sources, we were able to proceed by way of a "bootstrapping" process—a method introduced by psychologist Lawrence Kohlberg, which is characterized by triangulation from theory, research, and practice to create an interpretive frame and a set of specific recommendations. Obviously, our eclectic mix of sources does not provide the basis of a systematic empirical research project, but it does represent an ideal combination for a "grounded theory" that creates important distinctions, and for developing a frame for further theory, practice, and research.[3]

---

3. "Grounded theory" is a way of conducting research in waves, where each successive wave of data collection is used to shape and inform future waves. In this manner, theories evolve as part of the data collection process.

Chapter 1

Bridging Schools and Afterschool Programs

Chapter Overview

This chapter deals with linking afterschool programs to the school day, so that the different realms of learning reinforce one another. After justifying the importance of building bridges, we discuss ways of conceptualizing how afterschool programs connect to the school day. We then elaborate on the challenges to bridging, and recommend specific steps programs, researchers, funders, and schools might take to improve bridging conditions.

Why Bridge Afterschools and Schools?

The various environments youths inhabit can be conceptualized as multiple worlds with each environment having its own internal consistency (Noam, Pucci, & Foster, 1999). Phelan, Davidson, and Yu (1998) explain that the term *worlds* applies in this context because it indicates the "cultural knowledge and behavior found within the boundaries of students' particular families, peer groups, and schools" and, further, that "each world contains values and beliefs, expectations, actions, and emotional responses familiar to insiders" (p. 7). In other words, the culture of a child's school, afterschool program, community, and home can all be quite different, with different expectations for dress, behavior, speech, and so forth (Aikenhead, 1996; Au, 1980; Erickson & Mohatt, 1982; Heath, 1982; McLaughlin, 1993).

9

When the home and school worlds are congruous, development—especially academic development—is facilitated and the need for translation between these worlds is mitigated. Many studies have shown that when children's home and community cultures are continuous with school culture, their chances of achieving literacy and academic success are greatly enhanced when compared to their peers whose home and community worlds diverge from the school culture (Au & Mason, 1981; Delpit, 1995; Grant & Sleeter, 1996; Heath, 1982; Moll & Diaz, 1993; Phelan, Davidson, & Yu, 1998; Snow, Burns, & Griffin, 1998; Spindler, 1997). For example, Au (1980) found that, when reading lessons were adapted to reflect the cultural norms of native Hawaiian children, their reading achievement improved significantly in comparison to a control group that received traditional reading instruction. The advantage comes from the reinforcing effect that home and school cultures have on one another. Expectations for behavior and verbal expression become clearer, and the objective of lessons thereby becomes more meaningful, to participating children.

In contrast, when home and school cultures differ, schooling can increasingly appear confusing or irrelevant to many youth, thereby threatening their possibilities for achievement. As Gordon explains,

> The separation of affective from cognitive functions . . . is particularly senseless in the education of socially disadvantaged students. The social context in which education occurs is often alien for poor and minority students. Consequently, such students are less likely to be attracted, motivated or involved in the learning situation than more privileged kids for whom school has a more obvious relationship to the total context of their lives. (1979, p. 64)

Further, children whose home and community cultures conflict with school culture often feel as though they must choose to align themselves with one world, essentially provoking a choice between identities or a valuing of one culture over the other (see Davidson, 1999; Delgado-Gaitan, 1987; Erickson, 1993; John, 1972; Moll & Diaz, 1993; Ogbu, 1987; Spindler, 1997). Although current notions of good pedagogy suggest that school knowledge should incorporate students' "home languages, life experiences, and community backgrounds" (Grant & Sleeter, 1996, p. 233), implementing such pedagogy requires negotiating the competing demands of standards-based reform. Furthermore, the new immigration—which is the largest influx of immigrants since the beginning of the last century—makes incorporating the incredible diversity of students' languages, experiences, and communities a daunting challenge in and of itself.

An incongruity between home and school cultures, however, does not necessarily doom a child to failure. Snow and colleagues (Snow, Barnes, Chandler, Hemphill, & Goodman,1991) found that a sense of partnership between school and home is associated with gains in literacy achievement, regardless of ethnicity, income, and children's incoming abilities. In the study conducted by these researchers, the partnership usually involved parents and teachers exchanging information on the child's progress, both social and academic, throughout the year. Yet in the eyes of many minority parents, their relationships with schools often resemble a "confrontation" more than a collaboration, despite their own concerns and hopes for their children's education (Calabrese, 1990). Some cultural differences may be unbridgeable by a single person and require instead systematic training or institutional changes in order to be possible (Calabrese, 1990; Erickson & Mohatt, 1982). Another important source of connection between these worlds, however, is the afterschool experience.

Afterschool programs, by their very nature, tend to fall somewhere between the two worlds of home and school (whether they are congruous or not). Indeed, John and Leacock argue not only that "teaching and learning can take place outside as well as inside school walls," but also that they "can often take place better in the community" (1979, p. 88) precisely because that is where there is more continuity between children's worlds and learning. As such, afterschool can serve as a bridge between incongruous worlds, facilitating the transition between worlds and making choices between them seem less necessary. Moll and Diaz emphasize the role of afterschool and community-based settings as mediators, creating "strategic connections between schools and communities" (1993, p. 68). McLaughlin has found that community out-of-school programs describe their own success "primarily in terms of helping youth to achieve 'balance'—sure footing and sense of purpose—in their communities as well as an ability to negotiate different roles in different places—to draw on an array of features to give them several identities, all of which are anchored in a secure sense of self" (1993, p. 38).

In our own applied research we have used the term *bridging adolescent worlds* to express the attempt to foster a sense of continuity for youths as they traverse cultural contexts (Noam, Winner, Rhein, & Molad, 1996). Because they are informal, afterschool programs allow for in-depth adult-child relationships, can invite families and community to participate in programming, and have the ability to connect with schools; thus, they have the potential to function as a central environment connecting the multiple worlds of children (Noam, 2001; Noam et al., 1999). For instance, a key area of incongruity for many children, including Latino/as, Native Americans, and African Americans, is the individualistic and teacher-centered nature of most schooling in America, which contrasts with their cultures' valuing of group solidarity, interdependence, and collaboration (Au, 1980; Davidson, 1999; Erickson & Mohatt, 1982). The small group orientation of most afterschool programs makes learning endeavors more culturally relevant to such children. In fact, the simultaneous emphasis on relationships, fun, and learning found in so many afterschool programs is one of the key ways in which those programs can serve as a bridge between school and home cultures.

Modes of Bridging

In our initial efforts to understand bridging between schools and afterschool programs, we were struck by the lack of theoretical conceptualization on the topic. For that reason, we began our work by simultaneously collecting data and developing a productive typology of bridging, using Max Weber's approach to "ideal typing." Our typology describes the intensity of bridging in programs and remains neutral to the question of what type of intensity is "best." As we collected data through interviews and program visits, we found we needed to add to this typology in order to describe how differences in the intensity of bridging arise. This understanding is crucial to elaborating the challenges to bridging and to making recommendations for improving bridging. We organized our observations into:

three domains that specify the forms bridging can take
- interpersonal
- curricular
- systemic

four dimensions that articulate why and how programs bridge
- program location
- program philosophy of learning
- organizational capacity of programs and schools
- school climate

five types of bridging intensity that describe the closeness of the bridging relationship between schools and afterschools
- self-contained
- associated
- coordinated
- Integrated
- Unified

Domains of Bridging
Programs typically bridge within three domains: interpersonal, curricular, and systemic. Note that these domains are not mutually exclusive, but often are co-occurring. No matter what level or combination of levels is employed, bridging can be quite intense or less intense.

The most common domain we found was interpersonal bridging, which ranges from serendipitous meetings between school and afterschool personnel to regular contact between school and afterschool staff via telephone, email, and other means. Depending on what information is shared and how often, this level of bridging can have a positive impact on children socially, emotionally, and academically. The strength of the impact also depends upon whether the flow of information is reciprocal or one way. In many of our interviews, afterschool staff complained about the difficulty of establishing contact with busy school personnel.

The second domain of bridging we found was curricular bridging, which consists of attempted alignments between school and afterschool curricula. Curricular bridging focuses on supporting children academically, and it can occur as a result of other levels of bridging or quite separately from other bridging. Specifically, a program could achieve alignment referring to state standards rather than through interpersonal or systemic connections to schools. Compared to interpersonal bridging, the positive impact of curricular bridging depends less upon reciprocity and much more upon the clear articulation of goals and consistent development of curricula that engage and challenge children. The chapters that follow are devoted to homework and curricular choices, both of which can serve as curricular bridges between schools and afterschool programs.

Systemic bridging is the third domain of bridging we found. It involves formal collaboration between schools and afterschool programs, and entails sharing governance, funding, transportation, and systems between the two. For example, decisionmaking teams in both institutions might incorporate members from both institutions, insuring a certain level of collaboration. The meetings of such teams could range in their sphere of influence from the needs of individual children to future directions for the school and program. This domain of bridging has the potential to have a positive impact on children in multiple ways, but especially academically. The degree of impact seems to be determined by the respect accorded to each side by the other and by the commitment of both to truly collaborate.

Why Programs Bridge

The variation in the amount and type of bridging that afterschool programs implement with schools is inextricably linked to four factors: location, program philosophy, organizational capacity, and school climate. Location strongly influences bridging practices for obvious reasons. Programs located in schools have more opportunities for bridging than do programs in the community. School-based programs, even those that do not employ teachers, find it easier to access the curriculum, homework requirements, and general teaching styles of the school. Community-based programs—and school-based programs that accept children from other schools—must use more complex and labor-intensive means of communicating with

FIGURE1 *Domains of Bridging between School and Afterschool Programs*

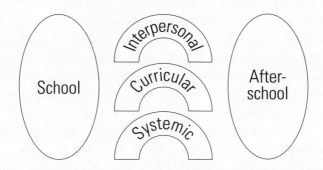

school personnel. Even so, we found that a program's location did not solely determine either the amount or type of bridging. In particular, just because a program is school based does not mean it necessarily bridges to any great degree. Instead, this variable interacted with the three others that affect bridging.

Program philosophy is the first of these additional variables. After-school programs vary considerably in their philosophies, especially in their philosophies of learning. While most stress informal contexts for learning, they differ in content and objectives. The subjects can range from content emphasized in school (e.g., reading, history, science, or math) to areas often minimally covered in school (e.g., art, drama, or music) to areas not typically covered before high school (e.g., sports, environmental education, or career exploration). In addition, regardless of subject(s), programs can vary in how well-defined their goals for learning are, ranging from clearly defined goals for children's learning to vague intentions. Finally, the programs may seek to reproduce, reinforce, supplement, or completely diverge from school goals. Even a program with explicit goals for academic learning may be conceived of as independent of school learning if its goals have no connection to school standards. Each of these aspects combines in forming a program's philosophy. Bridging is strongly affected by how closely the program leadership aligns its learning goals to school learning goals. Depending on the degree to which program leadership sees its learning goals as aligned to school learning goals, it will vary in whether and how it bridges between school and program.

Organizational capacity of programs also has an impact on bridging practices. Even a program that is located in a school and regards its learning goals as identical to the school's may not bridge very successfully as a result of insufficient organizational capacity. Programs vary in the time and resources they can commit to bridging. Capacity for bridging is closely tied to the number of staff who focus on this job responsibility and to the amount of competing responsibilities they have.

Finally, school climate affects how programs bridge. Bridging practices vary, depending on how program leaders and personnel perceive school quality and hence the desirability of bridging, and on how receptive school leadership and teachers are to program overtures. Multisite school-based programs may choose to bridge more with a school that is perceived as effective and welcoming and less with a school that is perceived as ineffective or unreceptive. School climate can have a particularly strong impact on bridging in community-based programs because they do not have the benefit of proximity that school-based programs have. In fact, location, program philosophy, organizational capacity, and school climate can separately or jointly enhance or constrain the intensity and form bridging takes in individual programs.

Bridging Intensity Typology

Considering both the domains of bridging and reasons behind them makes it possible to categorize programs according to the intensity of their relationships with schools. The following typology provides a scale of intensity from self-contained (programs and schools that do not interact interpersonally or organizationally) to unified (programs and schools that have been brought together in a "private school" model such that there is no distinction between the two institutions). Between these poles we distinguished three other types—associated, coordinated, and integrated— that represent a gradual increase in bridging intensity from one pole to the other. As we illustrate our bridging intensity typology with a few examples, many of the distinctions detailed above will also become clearer. We draw

FIGURE 2 *The Five Degrees of Bridging Intensity between Schools and Afterschool Programs*

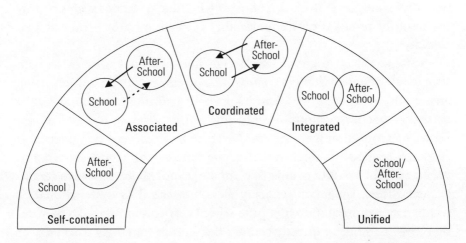

our examples from extensive research of and interviews with afterschool programs in Boston and Cambridge, Massachusetts, and across the country. The programs we have chosen to profile are not necessarily better or worse than other programs we consulted with or researched, but rather were chosen because they were particularly suited to distinctions we wished to elaborate for our readers.[1]

Self-Contained Programs

Programs that make little or no attempt to collaborate with schools we describe as self-contained. These programs usually have such a clearly defined mission that they perceive a stronger connection to schools to be potentially threatening, overwhelming, or simply unnecessary. As a result, the youth participants effectively constitute the only connection between school and afterschool. While some self-contained programs set aside a

---

1. It is important to note that some of the profiled programs are one of multiple sites. In these cases, we can speak with authority only about the specific program site where we interviewed. It is our experience that, although multisite programs usually share the same curriculum and philosophy, they can differ considerably in their levels of bridging.

block of time for homework, students tend to be responsible for using the time productively; such work is not regarded as connected to the true purpose of the program. The lack of bridging in these programs seems mainly the result of program philosophy rather than location or organizational capacity.

Self-contained programs tend to fall into two categories: those with strong, self-designed academic curricula, and those with a predominating arts, sports, or expeditionary learning focus. Interestingly, we found several programs that aim to promote academic learning, yet do not seek a high degree of connection with the school. These programs can be understood as "second schools"—intensive academic programs of study, delivered in the afterschool hours to compensate for the school's failure to reach certain students. These programs generally view the school as dysfunctional or children as requiring more than the school curriculum offers, so they design their methods to directly counter the schools' offerings. This view of the school explains why some of these programs do not reserve time for homework; others have such an ambitious curriculum that there simply is no time to spare.

We interviewed one such second school program located outside Massachusetts. The director described an openly hostile relationship with local schools, which he believed were intimidated by the success of his methods. This program did not include homework in its programming or attempt to extend the school's curriculum. Instead, the children from poor, inner-city neighborhoods received a challenging, "classical" curriculum, emphasizing literature, science, and second-language instruction. This program, like many of its peers, gave its own homework and assignments.

The Steppingstone program is another second school program operating in Boston and Philadelphia. Despite the location of the Boston-based program in a Boston public school, Steppingstone's philosophy keeps bridging at a minimum. Steppingstone's philosophy is that its "focused, demanding, result-oriented" environment and curriculum propels children to achieve in a way that the standard school curriculum does not (Steppingstone Foundation, n.d.). Its focus is for its scholars to apply to, be accepted into, and succeed at public "exam" schools and private schools. The fact that such schools demand more than simply meeting state standards means that the Steppingstone curriculum must go beyond the traditional school curriculum. The program is a rigorous one that requires a 14-month commitment from children, and its results are quite good, with 87 percent of the 2001 scholars getting into exam schools, and 90 percent of the 1995 scholars entering college in 2001.

Themed programs in arts, sports, or expeditionary learning also fall into this type because they tend to maintain minimal connections to the school's academic content. Many of these programs do not consider promoting academic competencies to be a meaningful part of their mission; instead, they focus on developing talent in other areas that the school has de-prioritized in favor of test prep. A recent survey of Massachusetts parents revealed that 45 percent of children "almost never participate in music, arts, or dancing programs" (Massachusetts 2020, 2002). Statistics of this sort demonstrate the significant void that themed programs can fill, and the need for them to maintain the integrity of their mission.

While programs in this category usually possess a strong justification for staying separate from the school, that decision often generates tension. As children get older, they require more rather than less academic help. Many parents and teachers insist that a program that takes place during the hours when children and teens characteristically do homework has an inherent responsibility to provide support in completing it. Also, as funding streams for afterschool become increasingly tied to academic objectives, themed programs often feel "pushed into a corner." In general, self-contained programs may compromise their own effectiveness if they become so alienated from the school that they cannot exchange information with teachers and guidance counselors about the overall well-being of children they jointly serve. Even so, it is clear from research that a great deal of high-quality learning that supplements the schools' curricula can take place in such programs if a program has well-articulated goals, a curriculum designed to meet those goals, and a staff capable of enacting that curriculum.

Associated Programs

We describe as associated those programs that reserve a role for school engagement in their program mission but do not have a strong connection to schools. We found that a major reason for the lack of strong connection was that schools have not been responsive to programs' attempts at outreach. The majority of programs we interviewed fell into this category. Community-based programs, in particular, often had this degree of bridging because of the added challenge that their locations presented to bridging efforts. At the same time, program philosophy and organizational capacity were also influential for both community- and school-based programs.

The specific technique(s) used to make contact with schools differed greatly from program to program, but tended to focus on interpersonal bridging. One popular method of outreach was sending surveys or forms to children's teachers that asked for information about academic strengths and weaknesses. Jenny Atkinson, senior director of education and arts for the Boys and Girls Clubs of America (BGCA), described a form that she used as a staff person at a club. It read: "This child has tutoring once per week. What areas should we focus on to make this time most effective?" (J. Atkinson, personal communication, August 1, 2001). While programs that use the same techniques might be regarded as having a higher intensity of bridging, what tended to distinguish the loose connection of associated programs to schools was that they typically experienced a limited response rate to surveys and other attempts at bridging.

Associated programs vary in the persistence with which they try to communicate with school personnel, according to the program's organizational capacity and philosophy. Programs that were more effective in this category achieved increased response rates by combining bridging methods. For example, a program staff person might follow up on written contact with informal contact in the form of the afterschool director introducing herself to the school principal(s) or engaging in some sort of outreach to teachers as well. Staff at the Oak Square YMCA in Boston, particularly the director of the school-age program, Terri Mulks, make an effort to have a presence in the schools by introducing themselves to teachers. They regularly send flyers and schedules to keep local schools abreast of events and activities at the program (T. Mulks, personal communication, October 15, 2001). As an example of another outreach technique, the B.E.L.L. Foundation, a school-based academic enrichment program, invites teachers to a reception at the beginning of the school year (P. Ogletree, personal communication, October 10, 2001).

Our interviews with program staff revealed that associated programs were limited in the intensity of their bridging because the onus for bridging tended to fall entirely on the programs. Many schools do not have a dedicated staff person to liaise with afterschool programs on a regular basis. Therefore, the responsibility to bridge falls on programs and on their staff, who must convince principals and teachers of the merit of collaborating with them.

Tim Garvin, vice president and executive director of the Boston YMCA, brought up another root cause for the limited intensity of associated programs: lack of time and resources (T. Garvin, personal communication, May 21, 2002). In the community-based YMCA programs, program directors are responsible for bridging, and that responsibility competes with a multitude of other, usually more pressing responsibilities that directly and immediately impact programs. When only one or two staff are responsible for bridging, and that responsibility represents only a small fraction of their responsibilities overall, bridging is destined to be limited. For instance, the Phillips Brooks House Association (PBHA), a student-run volunteer organization at Harvard, operates a number of afterschool programs in Boston and Cambridge. At their Mission Hill site, one of their oldest and most successful, the "clientele director" is the staff member responsible for bridging to both schools and families. As Varsha Ghosh, director of PBHA programs, explained, this dual responsibility, combined with the part-time and volunteer nature of the commitment (because the college student in this position inevitably has classes of her own to attend, which must take priority) inherently limits the amount of time a director can devote to bridging (V. Ghosh, personal communication, May 28, 2002).

In sum, although there was a basic familiarity between associated programs and schools, this did not necessarily translate into regular or deep sharing of information. The low intensity of bridging found in these programs was mainly due to limitations associated with location or organizational capacity or a combination of the two.

Coordinated Programs

Programs that maintain consistent communication with schools we describe as coordinated. The difference between a coordinated and associated program is primarily in organizational capacity. Both types share a program philosophy that considers engagement with schools to be an important factor in achieving learning goals. However, coordinated programs go a step further by dedicating significant staff time—50 percent or more, often at the director level—to liaising with schools. The efforts of this person or person(s) on staff allow for more elaborate bridging strategies to be employed, generally including interpersonal *and* curricular links.

We found that there is no consensus yet on the title of the person who performs these duties. She may be called the education coordinator at one program and the school liaison at another. Some programs do not specifically differentiate a position, but incorporate a significant amount of school contact or oversight of the educational component of a program into a staff member's existing role. In general, these individuals make regular contact with schools, have a broad understanding of the benchmarks that students in their program will have to achieve, and supervise direct-service staff in tutoring and programming to meet these educational needs.

The Jackson Mann Community Center After-School program (JMCC), located in the Allston neighborhood of Boston, is an example of successful interpersonal and curricular bridging effected by an education coordinator. The education coordinator of the school-based program is a familiar face in the school. With the approval of the principal, she is able to greet teachers informally as she walks through the halls or picks up children at the end of the day. She distributes a brief survey to teachers at the beginning of the year requesting information about the strengths and weaknesses of children in her program, then follows up with teachers in person to ensure they are filled out and returned. Due to her relationship with teachers, the return rate is as high as 90 percent. The education coordinator uses this data on individual children to guide the work of the college student volunteer tutors whom she supervises, and to inform her decisions when purchasing games and educational supplements for the program. She also has access to the children's grades and uses that as another informational and evaluative tool.

It should be noted that this level of intensity also applies to programs that make use of a curriculum that is strongly aligned with school-related benchmarks. We have seen programs that are coordinated in spite of the fact that they do very little interpersonal bridging with school personnel. This may be because the program is located in the community, serves children from different schools, operates multiple sites, or simply does not have the organizational capacity to support liaising activities. Instead, these programs have chosen to bridge curricularly by implementing a package or self-designed curriculum that is both suited to the afterschool context and standards-based.

Citizen Schools, creative afterschool programs with headquarters in Boston, has two curricular approaches to bridging. One is their innovative apprenticeship model that brings together disadvantaged middle school youth and local professionals to complete a project. Past apprenticeships have ranged from performing a mock trial at a city courthouse facilitated by lawyers and a real judge to creating a cookbook with a chef. Academic competencies are taught as they relate to completing the project. Additionally, Citizen Schools implements a literacy curriculum at all 13 Boston sites, called the Writing and Data Project, which is aligned with Boston Public School standards. These projects require students to do research, analyze and write about it, and present their conclusions. For example, a group of students from Citizen Schools at one Boston school explored their values and where they come from in a project called In Your Hands. The students worked on their narrative writing skills, a sixth-grade standard in Massachusetts, by writing personal essays and publishing them in a book.

A common challenge coordinated programs face is that, while there exists a fairly intense desire to support the school curriculum, the two institutions of afterschool and school are still essentially separate. They interface through the designated liaison or a part of the afterschool curriculum that is aligned with state standards. Nonetheless, the majority of the staff at the program is uninvolved directly with bridging efforts. This is not necessarily a disadvantage, because it does free most staff from the considerable effort required to work with schools; at the same time, it will affect the degree to which all members of the staff can fully reinforce or complement school-day learning.

Integrated Programs

Programs that engage in a systemic or institutional relationship with schools we describe as integrated. At this level of bridging, both the program and the school have identified the other as a key partner in achieving their goals around learning and other aspects of development. Additionally, the afterschool program develops an organizational structure that will allow it to devote staff time and resources to interpersonal, curricular, and institutional bridging, with reciprocal investments on the side of the school. The afterschool program and school share space, staff, and procedures. Clear curricular continuities exist. An afterschool director may obtain a grant for equipment (e.g., computers) that directly benefits the day program, or the two institutions may apply for grants collaboratively. Administrative structures support shared goal-setting and the easy flow of information back and forth. Two important indicators that a program is integrated are that the afterschool director is a part of the school leadership team and that school personnel are on the program's advisory board. Certainly, not every integrated program will exemplify each of these traits. We identify programs as being of this intensity type because they have deep structures that support bridging, which are systemic and fairly permanent.

RALLY, a program developed by faculty at the McLean Hospital and Harvard Graduate School of Education (HGSE), exemplifies the integrated bridging type (e.g., Noam, Pucci, & Foster, 1999). RALLY, which stands for Responsive Advocacy for Life and Learning in Youth, is an in-school/afterschool academic and mental health intervention at the Taft Middle School in Allston-Brighton and the Grover Cleveland Middle School in Dorchester, both in Massachusetts. The program has developed a new professional role called "prevention practitioners." These practitioners are youth development specialists who bring together knowledge of education, community development, and mental health practices. Practitioners work in classrooms during the school day, two days per week, providing academic and behavioral support to the whole class and extra services to children identified as being particularly at risk. The practitioners run discussion groups with kids and work with parents to locate clinicians or other social services when needed. These supports extend into the nonschool hours because practitioners staff their own on-site RALLY afterschool program for students they work with during the day, which carries over the focus on academic and mental health resiliency but with different methods. Teachers also participate in the afterschool program. While the classroom and afterschool programs require close collaboration between teachers and prevention practitioners, incorporating RALLY into the school has necessitated collaboration at the management level. RALLY is a part of the school support and leadership teams. This integrated approach provides continuities for the "whole" child and yields benefits for learning.

The Transition to Success Project Pilot is another Boston program currently operating in six middle schools, which involves school and afterschool programs in helping to improve the academic performance of academically at-risk students. The creative design involves in-depth collaboration among schools, afterschool programs, and community organizations. It represents a collaborative model and has produced a successful set of pilots led by full-time coordinators. Although some of the pilots have yet to reach the level of integration that the coordinators believe is necessary to support students (Davis & Farbman, 2002), the model is a strong one, and we believe that further integration will occur with time.

Full-service schools such as Children's Aid Society community schools or, locally, Boston EXCELs and the Gardner Elementary School in Allston provide other models of the integrated bridging type. The Gardner is a Community Learning Center that has developed partnerships with the YMCA and Boston College. The principal considers the afterschool program to be a vital part of the whole school, and aspires to have every student enrolled in it. The afterschool program provides children with a wide range of opportunities from homework help to painting and karate. Since the adoption of this community school approach, the students' standardized test scores have shown one of the highest rates of improvement in the state (Davis & Farbman, 2002).

Unified Programs
Unified programs are at the opposite end of the bridging continuum from self-contained programs and represent the greatest degree of bridging. Unified programs are essentially indistinguishable from school because they are on-site and are part of a truly extended school day. The extended

day in this intensity of bridging does not mean that school has wholly infiltrated afterschool. Instead, the day incorporates the best of both worlds and weaves them together seamlessly.

We did not discover any programs in Boston or New York that closely fit this description. Although there are some private schools that organize their school day in this manner, we did not have the opportunity to interview any of them. Despite the fact that this type of bridging has not been tested in public schools, the potential of such programs is strong. Rick Weissbourd, co-founder of ReadBoston and a lecturer at HGSE, maintains that the extended day model, or unified bridging type, would allow schools to provide a schedule that reflects the "natural rhythms of children" at different ages (R. Weissbourd, personal communication, June 24, 2002). De Kanter, Huff, and Chung (2002) contend that such a model would enable schools to address subjects that have been increasingly viewed as supplemental or peripheral to their academic goals. In essence, the thinkers who support this level of intensity as both possible and desirable contend that afterschool could infect both the spirit and content of typical schooling, thereby better meeting the needs of every child. It remains to be seen whether this vision can be realized in public schools and whether it will be successful in cross-pollinating the purposes and methods of school and afterschool.

Challenges

In almost every case, the program staff we interviewed and observed wanted to connect to and communicate with the children's teachers. The most commonly cited barrier to such bridging was a misunderstanding or underestimation by teachers of the role of afterschool. Program staff often noted that teachers seem to regard afterschool programs as places of mere recreation, and one program director said that his attempts to confer with teachers about the children were met with great suspicion, as though he was "looking over their backs." Another program director believed that teachers consider afterschool staff to be unnecessary middlemen. Jenny Atkinson from Boys and Girls Clubs of America described having to challenge the teachers' perception of the club as "gym and swim" (J. Atkinson, personal communication, August 1, 2001). Our interviews reveal that efforts at bridging are almost entirely one-sided, with the effort always starting with the program rather than the school, even in instances of more intense bridging (coordinated and integrated).

Many programs that seek to establish deep integration with the school day are developing innovative models toward that end. While progress is being made, it will be a long road to build real consensus, or even to achieve compromise. At a recent conference on afterschool sponsored by Julius Wilson at Harvard University's Kennedy School of Government, many participants were vocal in their disbelief that teachers and school administrators are either willing or able to develop new educational strategies appropriate in the afterschool context. Since the 21st Century Community Learning Center grants no longer require application through a school system, we may soon see marked shifts in goal-setting, governance, perception, and control of afterschool, steering a course away from reliance on the methods and goals of the school day.

Not all obstacles to bridging are ideological; there also exist significant practical barriers. Afterschool programs eager to establish connections with schools may lack the full-time staff needed to create those connections. For programs lacking full-time staff, few bridging options are available. The Boys and Girls Club of Somerville, Massachusetts, for example, serves two hundred active members—children who come from seven different elementary schools and three middle schools—yet the club employs only one full-time program staff member, effectively precluding any meaningful interpersonal bridging effort. Lack of time on the part of teachers is also cited often as a major barrier to establishing connections between teachers and program staff.

Of special note here is the issue of using school teachers as afterschool staff. Such a model has the built-in possibility of achieving integrated bridging, often with less difficulty than is experienced by programs run by community-based organizations, whether they are in or outside of schools. However, such programs also face the risk of making school and afterschool indistinguishable from one another. If the school in question is innovative, and achieves a strong level of learning, then such overlapping presents no problem. But if the school is struggling to meet productive levels of teaching and learning, the very qualities that underachieving and underserved youth find most alienating about school may find their way into afterschool: an authoritarian tone, a drill-and-kill approach, and a lack of stimulating options based on children's interests and choices. The regimented nature and controlling tone of some of our classrooms must be avoided in an afterschool context (and, of course, such practices should also be changed during the school day).

Furthermore, it may be too much to ask teachers to take on the job of a youth development worker when they already have a very demanding job. Successful afterschool work requires skills in conflict resolution, counseling, curriculum design, and developmental psychology. In order to assist children as they navigate through the domains of school, home, and community, afterschool practitioners need familiarity with academic curriculum, an understanding of the cultural milieu, and a significant store of local knowledge, or what one program administrator refers to as a "Ph.D. in the Streets" (Roberto Colon, cited in McLaughlin, Irby, & Langman, 1994, p. 133). Practitioners face the challenge of negotiating delicate relationships with youth in settings that provide less support and structure than schools, and "knowledge of what youth go through in the networks and neighborhoods in which they live" (McLaughlin et al., 1994, p. 133) is an invaluable tool in this endeavor. Thus, the ability to traverse multiple worlds is not only something that programs help children do, but also something that staff members at the program must practice themselves.

Still, even among the associated programs whose efforts were often the most frustrated, bridging was regarded as crucial. As one director noted, "we are the mediums" (M. Tempesta-Rios, personal communication, October 18, 2001). Helping teachers and school administrators recognize the crucial role programs play, both in supporting school aims and in connecting to families in ways not available to schools, is a critical challenge to the successful linking of schools and afterschools. Until administrators endorse programs as legitimate partners in supporting children academically and socially, true collaborative bridging cannot exist. The lack of endorsement from administrators and teachers can stymie bridging at every level.

Recommendations

In the past year, the Boston Afterschool for All Partnership invited us to produce a research and policy paper with recommendations on how to enhance bridging in order to increase learning. Many of the recommendations described here have found their way into action plans in Boston. Our recommendations offer specific ways of addressing the issue of bridging at a systems level. We do not discount the innumerable ways that program staff can connect with teachers and principals on an interpersonal level. Indeed, many of the practitioners we interviewed in associated, coordinated, and integrated programs described the "small things"—saying hello in the hallways or at pick-up points, or initiating written communication through a survey or letter—as being essential to the bridging process. Nonetheless, our recommendations primarily focus on the larger information-dissemination, training, and funding systems. Note that we are not suggesting that bridging schools and afterschools is more important than, or should be done to the exclusion of, reaching out to parents and the community. On the contrary, it is our vision that afterschools can serve as the place where the multiple worlds that children inhabit meet in a non-competitive way that supports their growth as whole human beings.

Program Recommendations

Assessing Program Goals and Capacity

Clearly, the first step for any program seeking to improve bridging is to evaluate how the program's goals and organizational capacity align with bridging goals. A school-based or community-based program with a strong recreational focus and few academic priorities likely will have less need to confer with teachers about achievement issues than a school-based extended day program. By the same token, a program staffed primarily by volunteers may not possess the capacity both to collect information from teachers and to convert it into meaningful program content. Given the time and resource constraints programs generally face, no program director should make elaborate efforts to reach out just for the sake of doing so.

Programs should engage in bridging with purposefulness and logic, apportioning their effort and methods to their mission.

Professional Development for Afterschool Staff

Afterschool practitioners generally benefit from training designed to enhance their knowledge of school curricula, homework, and testing requirements. Many agencies have begun to conduct trainings that help programs articulate and plan the learning content of activities in terms of statewide standards. We encourage continued efforts in this direction.

At a minimum, afterschool programs should require school visits as part of their staff's initial orientation and training. Such visits give staff invaluable insight into the environment in which their children spend the early part of the day, and reinforce both in perception and reality the role of afterschool in promoting academic achievement. Besides bringing the program into the school, the school should also be brought into the program, as appropriate. Teachers and administrators should be invited not only to open houses and culminating events at the program, but also to visit and join in during daily operations. Tom Regan, director of afterschool programs at the Jackson Mann Community Center and other sites in Allston-Brighton, favors hiring school-day paraprofessionals as afterschool staff because of their ready knowledge of children, teachers, and school curriculum (T. Regan, personal communication, October 4, 2001). When school faculty is invited into the afterschool context as visitors or regular participants, they have the opportunity to see how children play and perform in a different setting.

School Recommendations

Professional Development for School Staff

We believe a set of trainings parallel to those we recommend for afterschool staff is necessary for teachers, specifically about youth development and teaching techniques in the out-of-school hours. We should not presume that teachers naturally know how to function in the afterschool setting, even if the program occurs in the same building. If school-day teachers are to work in afterschool, they need training and ongoing support in order to be able to cultivate what is different and indeed best about afterschool teaching, including working with children in smaller groups, managing behavior in new ways, trying different curricular approaches, and building relationships with children that do not center on academics. Schools of education should expose preservice teachers to afterschool programs so that they are poised to participate in these programs effectively. Also, school administrators may require training to develop their skills in collaborating with afterschool personnel and directors.

Workshops for Principals

Our work with The After-School Corporation (TASC) in New York City, an initiative of George Soros' Open Society Institute (board chairman is Herb Sturz; Lucy Friedman is president), has proven that training and workshops can contribute dramatically to bridging. We have been encouraged about the possibilities for partnership between schools and afterschools by our two-year collaboration with TASC, where we developed training workshops and conferences for school principals who host afterschool programs in their buildings.[2] In the first year of our efforts, many principals tended to demonstrate one of two basic attitudes toward the afterschool programs they managed jointly with community-based organizations (CBOs). One group conceived of their programs as an extension of the school day, despite their partnership with community-based organizations. The other group adopted an attitude of benign neglect toward the programs, feeling that they had done their part by simply providing space. The principals in the first group commonly used a language of control and ownership, and they saw themselves as overseers and caretakers of programs that represented to them a serious responsibility (a common remark we heard was, "I am in charge of everything in my building"). The principals in the second group shared the basic assumptions of those in the first group even while remaining aloof. After the second year of our collaboration, however, we witnessed a dramatic change in attitude. A growing number of principals now spoke of a collaborative effort with the afterschool director, describing

2. This collaboration also included the Principals' Center at the Harvard Graduate School of Education. A third conference, jointly sponsored by TASC and PAER, was held in New York City in April 2002.

regular meetings, systemic collaboration, and the development of mutual trust and shared goals inspired by a vision of schools, community-based organizations, and cultural institutions working together. Issues of power, control, and responsibility were subsumed by excitement about a collaborative effort some principals describe as a "marriage." This shift in the attitude of principals and their ways of conceptualizing the work of afterschool programs illustrates the differences among types of programs in our model, and clearly shows how improvements in bridging can be supported by convening leaders and providing training.

We therefore recommend ongoing meetings with principals in Boston, Cambridge, and other communities nationwide looking to strengthen bridging. Rather than demanding that afterschool should take on school practices, we emphasize training for both program leaders and school leaders and efforts from both sides to make bridging successful. Efforts should not be made solely in the area of workshops and training, but should also involve organizational shifts by which school leaders invite afterschool leaders into the academic management and decisionmaking system. In many schools, appointing the afterschool director to the school leadership team represents a significant turning point in the school/afterschool relationship. Resources and communication must constantly flow both ways in order to ensure that organizational inclusion of afterschool proves productive for all parties. Similarly, afterschool staff and leaders require training, supervision, and consultation if they are to function productively in the school and to become partners of teachers and administrators.

School/Parent/Program Liaison

One promising school practice some of our interviewees spoke of was the "parent liaison" that exists in some Boston schools. Although this person's job is nominally to connect parents and schools, according to a number of our interviewees, this person also sometimes serves as a link between schools and programs. It is this link we wish to encourage. Since the liaison job already requires the ability to bridge home and school worlds, to forge relationships with families, and to convey a "sense of what school is like" to outsiders, this person seems a natural candidate for afterschool bridging efforts (J. Caplan, personal communication, June 25, 2002). A similar position exists in the Boston YMCA programs that are school based, indicating that there is potential for this sort of position either in schools or in programs. Even so, with a more secure funding base than programs typically have, schools may be the more appropriate place for such a crucial position.

Funding Recommendations

Strengthened and Continuing Collaboration Between Schools and CBOs

This particular recommendation stems from concerns raised by the recent change in the 21st Century Community Learning Center grant-making system. We believe it is crucial that schools and CBOs continue down the path of collaboration upon which they have recently embarked. Some of the most exciting models we have witnessed in our research involved school-CBO partnerships. It would be a shame to see such innovation stymied by a lack of funding incentives for schools and CBOs to work closely together. Jennifer Davis, president of Massachusetts 2020, makes a strong argument that bridging "is not just an issue of individuals schools or programs" but that it needs to be addressed systemically, with policies that create incentives and resources for collaboration (J. Davis, personal communication, December 15, 2001). Judy Caplan of the North Central Regional Laboratory in Naperville, Illinois, told us of such an initiative in Chicago that gives $1,500 grants to teachers to conceive afterschool projects that could support their curriculum (J. Caplan, personal communication, June 25, 2002). Dishon Mills of the Boston Public Schools suggested that "cross-fertilization" grants, which foster teacher and afterschool personnel collaboration in curriculum planning, are another important way such bridging could be encouraged systemically (D. Mills, personal communication, June 25, 2002). In addition, issues of space sharing, transportation, and training cannot be left just to the initiative of partners, but require a new set of policies. We recommend that funders allot significant resources to expanding productive bridging practices and collaborative efforts between schools and communities.

Funding for an Afterschool Staff Presence in Schools

We recommend strongly that funds be made available to foster an after-school staff presence in schools during the school day. Rather than focusing on collaboration solely at the leadership level, we advocate collaboration at a teacher and staff level as well. Adriana de Kanter gave voice to these concerns when she argued that afterschool personnel really need "to get to know what takes place during the school year," especially in terms of curriculum, so that they are better able to support learning by developing meaningful and integrated hands-on activities and field trips that enrich school-day learning (A. de Kanter, personal communication, November 15, 2001). Having staff observe and assist in classrooms during the regular school day will also give them a better sense of school practices and the challenges their youth face during the day. Such a presence will facilitate the transition from school to afterschool time, and will have the added benefit of bringing a youth development perspective into the classroom and an academic perspective into the afterschool program.

It is essential for the success of bridging efforts to set up ongoing training and convene discussions between afterschool staff and teachers. Collaboration requires systematic and compensated support, which most programs will not be able to afford without outside funding. It is also important to fund sites willing to serve as demonstration and training centers. This type of hands-on training, which includes site-based observations, will prove an essential complement to ongoing workshops and seminars.

Resource Clearinghouse

We recommend that in areas with a large number of afterschool programs, particularly urban centers like Boston and Cambridge, resource clearing-houses be established. These centers would offer programs and their staff a centralized source for professional development and assistance in bridging and standards-aligned curriculum development. These centers might also provide the training for teachers who work in afterschool programs. Such a clearinghouse would ease the demands made on programs and schools and could further promote bridging across programs.

Research and Evaluation Recommendations

A National Catalog of Sample Bridging Practices

A national catalog of sample bridging practices, setting out the variety of means currently used to connect afterschool and school and serving as a resource for educators, would offer us an invaluable comprehensive understanding of the challenges programs face and creative solutions for them. Such a catalog seems to us a requisite first step for evaluating the efficacy of different modes of bridging across varied contexts. As Darlene Currie has pointed out, to improve learning in programs, we need to seek out "best ingredients of success" rather than only focus on model programs, because no one program gets everything right (D. Currie, personal communication, October 12, 2001). Although we at PAER have begun to assemble such a list of practices, small and large, a systematic national scan is needed.

Research and Evaluation

Careful research should be conducted to compare the outcomes of different forms of bridging. Ideally, the choices made in afterschool programming of whether and how to bridge to schools should be based on data drawn from comparative studies, rather than on instinct, belief, or ideology. As for how to conduct this research, those interviewees we spoke with about evaluation tended to argue for both qualitative and quantitative methods. In addition to following easily traceable outcomes, such as attendance, grades, and test scores, instruments measuring more specific outcomes need to be developed. The problem with outcomes that are easily tracked is that they are global measures and tend not to capture the qualitative changes that children undergo during participation in a successful afterschool program. Hence, it seems advisable that, in addition to quantitative tools, a fine-grained qualitative description of programs' effects could yield important insight into what outcomes are most likely to show change and for which sorts of programs.

Chapter 2

Extended Learning

School Content through Homework Support

Chapter Overview

In this chapter we consider and discuss homework's place in afterschool. After justifying the importance of homework to afterschool learning, we describe the patterns in homework practices that we found in our research, review challenges cited in interviews, and conclude by offering specific recommendations for improving homework practices.

Why Discuss Homework in a Book on Learning in Afterschool?

Out-of-school time is, of course, the traditional time in which homework gets done. It seems inevitable that if children are in programs for three or more hours a day, they will either need to do their homework in the program or at home. Given that parents of children in afterschool programs do not see their children until 5 P.M. or 6 P.M. and have dinner and family matters to which they must attend, it should not surprise us that parents who send their children to an afterschool program typically expect that they will have completed all, or at least a large part, of the homework assigned for the night at the afterschool (e.g., O'Connor & McGuire, 1998; Youth Development Institute, 1997). Boston-area parents ranked homework support as the most desired aspect of afterschool programming (Bain & Company,

1998). A recent survey also reveals that a great majority of parents feel that extra tutoring in afterschools will help their children develop the skills necessary to succeed (Massachusetts 2020, 2002). Moreover, according to a number of programs and leaders we interviewed, many parents enroll their children in afterschool programs with the intention of receiving help for their children's homework that they themselves do not feel capable of providing due to educational, linguistic, or other barriers. Most teachers and principals we have worked with in our demonstration sites in Boston, as well as in our consultation and training efforts, mention homework support as an essential aspect of any successful program. The youth with whom we have worked, particularly middle school students, also view homework help as an important reason why they attend programs.

Although there is a body of research on homework, very little research exists with a specific focus on homework in afterschool programs. We were able to locate only one report on this topic, published by the National Institute of Out-of-School Time (NIOST): a broad survey of various stakeholders' positions on homework and of afterschool homework practices that offers an enlightening discussion of the pros and cons of the latter (O'Connor & McGuire, 1998). To find more research, we turned to the general body of homework research. Drawing upon nine studies that correlate homework with school achievement, Cooper (1989, cited in Cooper, 2001a) found that beyond the one- to two-hour mark the achievement of middle school students no longer correlates significantly with the time spent on homework. Only for high school students do the correlations continue beyond the two-hour mark; for elementary students there is no significant correlation at all. Even though no significant relationship has been found between elementary students' achievement and any amount of homework, Cooper advises that homework in moderation is still important for elementary students because it helps them "develop good study habits and grow as their cognitive capacities mature" (Cooper, 2001b, p. 37). Although many critics of homework disagree with homework advocates over whether homework is beneficial to elementary and middle school children, such arguments tend to concentrate on the disruption of home life. In fact, at least one vehement critic of homework argues that if homework must be given, its place is in afterschool programs, where staff other than teachers can support children's learning (Kralovec & Buell, 2000). Although Kralovec and Buell (2000) argue that such practices should be restricted to older students (from middle school onward), they value the individualized help that programs can offer and that parents might not be able to give.

Despite the lack of conclusive evidence of homework's positive effect on academic achievement in lower grades, completion of homework undeniably affects children's grades for homework itself in school. In addition, there is a growing body of evidence that afterschool programs help produce academic achievement and motivational gains, although to what extent such gains are attributable to homework help is still unclear (Posner & Vandell, 1994, 1999; L. Reisner, personal communication, October 25, 2001; Schinke, Cole, & Poulin, 2000). Additionally, the fact is that today in Boston 96 percent of afterschool programs already address homework in their programming (Children's Museum & Boston 2:00-to-6:00 Initiative, 2000), up from 80 percent in 1998 (Bain & Company, 1998). Thus, given that homework help is already demanded and provided in afterschool programs, we do not engage in the larger debate of homework's efficacy in promoting academic achievement. Rather, we focus on tracing homework practices in afterschool programs and offer specific recommendations for how to incorporate effective homework help and support children's academic learning while protecting the traditionally more relaxed climate of afterschool.

Homework Practices

In refining our thinking about homework practices, we turned to our interviews with afterschool programs. The majority of program staff we interviewed incorporated homework into their programming, and the bulk of those placed homework at the beginning of the afterschool day, often after a brief snack period. Beyond these commonalities, there was a great deal of variety in homework practices, with programs varying in how they grouped students, how much time was devoted to it, how many adults were present for assistance, and in many other important aspects of implementation. Furthermore, while most programs incorporated homework as a regular part of the afterschool, some programs chose to provide no time for home-work at all, and still others made participation voluntary. Surprisingly, we did not find the range of practices delineated in a detailed report by O'Connor and McGuire (1998). Instead, we found that we could more meaningfully capture the differences among programs by identifying dif-ferent approaches toward homework. In the end, we distinguished three different approaches:

1. homework as task completion
2. homework as an opportunity to build relationships and target tutoring
3. homework as an inspiration for enriched learning activities

It is through these distinctions that we were able to better understand di-verse program practices and arrived at our recommendations.

Homework as Task Completion
Programs where homework was viewed primarily as a task to be completed were characterized by a pragmatic attitude. In general, programs with this perspective speak of homework in concrete, task-oriented terms. Further, homework in these programs is a stand-alone activity that does not connect to the rest of the programming day. It is almost as if, once homework is completed or the appointed time is up, the real afterschool program be-gins. Finally, programs that considered homework a duty to be fulfilled as quickly and painlessly as possible tended to utilize larger and sometimes random groups with a higher children-to-adult ratio than in the other two approaches to homework delineated below.

Programs that used this approach kept homework completely separate from other programming. In one instance, an opening ritual that is used to mark the beginning of the afterschool day did not actually occur until after homework had been completed. In other programs, homework was re-served for a time after other programming more central to the program goals had been completed. Along similar lines, one middle school in Ohio required students who wished to participate in clubs and athletics after school to give proof of participation in an hour-long afterschool home-work or academic session. To facilitate this practice, no extracurricular activity began until after the academic sessions were over, and the school further offered a homework center as one of the extracurricular activities for those needing extra time and help to complete their assignments (Glazer & Williams, 2001). Thus, while homework was a priority, it remained separate from other afterschool options. In programs like these, the main goal of homework time is simply to complete assignments so that children can devote their time to their own interests, friends, and family. Interestingly, many very high-quality programs in Boston and Cambridge fall into this category.

Homework as Opportunity for Relationship and Skill Building

In contrast to programs that saw homework merely as a task to be completed, programs that regarded homework as an opportunity for relationship and skill building actively worked to make homework time more productive for children. Homework in these programs was seen, at least to some extent, as a mentoring opportunity. These programs felt the quality of homework help sessions depended largely upon the relationships that staff and volunteers built with the children during homework time. Good relationships included consistent expectations for completing homework, but extended beyond this to generating positive effects among children and staff. Indeed, staff members who had developed their own routines, high expectations, and positive relationships with youths were viewed as the most successful by several program directors (e.g., M. Farley, personal communication, July 11, 2001; L. Van Dyken, personal communication, July 5, 2001; L. Warner, personal communication, July 5, 2001). Programs that valued and wished to foster these relationships tended to prefer an adult working with children in groups kept as small as possible, with groups and relationships remaining consistent over time. Furthermore, such small groups and good relationships made it easier to identify children experiencing great difficulty completing homework, which might lead to referral for one-on-one tutoring to strengthen weak skills. Despite the more integrated inclusion of homework in these programs, the end goal of homework remained largely the same as for those programs that viewed homework as a task to be completed, though these programs went a step further by trying to create a more nurturing atmosphere of individualized and relationship-oriented homework support. One characteristic program of this latter sort, the Fanueil Afterschool Program, grouped three children consistently with the same adult. Children who experienced particular difficulty with homework were paired with volunteers who attended the program every day to promote the greatest consistency possible in both tutelage and the relationship between volunteers and the children. Children were tracked through homework logs, and their success was monitored not only in terms of completion, but also in terms of skills, attention, following directions, and industriousness. If children finished their homework before homework time was up or before others in their group had finished, they engaged in educational activities such as reading, writing, coloring, or playing computer or board games. This approach signaled to the children that the aim of homework was not only completing homework, but also using homework to build relationships and skills.

Homework as Springboard to Enrichment

While programs that regarded homework as an opportunity for relationship and skill building worked to make homework time more productive than simple task completion, programs that regarded homework as a springboard to enrichment used homework as a tool for broader program goals. In these programs, homework completion was almost a by-product of the larger purpose of promoting a love of learning and academic achievement. These programs aimed at not only completed homework, good relationships, and skill building, but also at innovative activities based on homework that extended learning beyond the assignment. Examples of this approach to homework are the Boys and Girls Clubs of America's Power Hour and Work Family Directions' Homework and Edutainment Club (Work Family Directions [WFD], 2000).

The Power Hour is the homework and tutoring component of the Boys and Girls Clubs of America's learning strategy called Project Learn. It has three components: homework help, tutoring, and enrichment activities, also called Power Pages. The Power Hour is a daily ritual that takes place at a consistent time in a space stocked with school supplies and supplemental reference materials to inculcate good homework habits. Staff are encouraged not merely to supervise the room but actively to assist children. Students work in cooperative groups, with tutors, especially volunteers from local colleges and universities, available to provide one-on-one assistance with difficult concepts. If members complete their homework before the Power Hour is over, club staff will direct them to Power Pages, which are technology or paper-based enrichment activities that reinforce skills from school. For example, students might explore a topic of interest on the Encarta Africana CD-ROM. Power Points are an incentive system that rewards children for participating in the three elements of Power Hour. Children can redeem points for books, supplies, or field trips.

In the case of the Homework and Edutainment Club, learning is extended through a variety of means.[1] Staff from programs using this approach are trained not just in addressing homework and using it to create extended learning opportunities, but also in establishing a child-centered atmosphere, where homework is completed in an environment as home-like as possible, which includes both formal and informal spaces conducive to both individual and small group work. The homework space also includes a plethora of reference materials, resources, and supplies that are developmentally appropriate for the youth served by the program. Ideally, the space is designed and decorated by staff and youth working together, giving them a stronger sense of ownership. Furthermore, through such training, staff work to change their own and children's perspectives on homework and academic learning. Children provide information in a survey that allows them and staff to understand their individual learning styles. Through the training, afterschool staff learn to bring topics alive and help children with difficult concepts through use of reference materials (such as dictionaries, thesauruses, atlases, and encyclopedias) and manipulatives (including puzzles, games, and flashcards), all of which are ideally chosen in response to a child's strengths and learning styles. For instance, imagine that a child is having difficulty understanding the multiple causes of the Civil War. Staff might help elucidate the matter through reading an encyclopedia entry, visiting online websites that offer multimedia curricular options, or acting out key events through role-playing, depend-

1. Our discussion of the Homework and Edutainment Club was informed considerably by an interview with Robert Weinstein of The After-School Corporation (personal communication, August 8, 2001).

ing on whether a child is most responsive to linguistic, spatial and/or musical, or kinesthetic learning.

Finally, children participate in their own homework and academic goal-setting, again giving them more ownership. Perhaps the most important ingredient to an approach like this is the belief that homework can and should be fun for children. The interest and engagement generated in a homework topic might be further explored through projects inspired by the extended consideration prompted by this sort of extended learning.

Challenges

While three different overall approaches to homework characterize programs we interviewed, there were interesting continuities in the challenges reported. We discovered a number of barriers that challenged programs to offer optimal homework help. The three most common barriers cited by programs and leaders alike were problems encountered in using volunteers, distinguishing the goals of homework and tutoring (and finding time for both), and a lack of resources.

Most common among the challenges cited was the difficulty of using volunteers, usually drawn from the rich assortment of local colleges and universities. While volunteers were a resource clearly valued by programs and leaders (and were in fact desired in greater numbers by many programs), a variety of drawbacks to volunteer use were cited in interviews. A perceived lack of consistency in attendance, experience, and ability among student volunteers was a major challenge. One program, for example, noted that volunteers who served solely as tutors had a tendency to remain aloof from the staff and the rest of the program day. Another program felt inadequate at matching tutors and children. Yet another program explained that training was needed in behavioral management and computer use. The issue is complicated further when a program relies on high school, rather than undergraduate, tutors, as the MissionSAFE program in Mission Hill does. The object at the MissionSAFE program is not only to obtain tutors for the program, but to provide teenagers with a meaningful experience and a chance to act as role models. Although this and many other programs find inherent value in the use of younger tutors, others in the field worry about teenagers' ability to handle such responsibility, particularly when it is tied to academic support. Opinion among programs was divided on whether volunteer college students required training in providing homework help. While some felt college enrollment was enough of a guarantee that tutors would understand content, others argued that volunteers needed training in how to help without giving away answers, how to use children's confusions to guide learning, and how to build creative and engaging lessons and relationships. At least one study has demonstrated that, with proper training, undergraduate tutors improve not only their tutees' skills (in this case literacy skills), but also their own (Juel, 1996).

A related barrier to effective homework time noted by both programs and other interviewees was the inherent tension between tutoring and homework help. Despite parental and school pressure to complete homework, the directors of these programs felt volunteers valued one-on-one tutoring over more general homework help, and the directors themselves seemed to feel tutoring was the more effective and rewarding experience. Afterschool leaders argued that homework and tutoring need to be distinguished more clearly in many programs. Those we interviewed felt that the lack of clear intentions for and distinctions between homework and tutoring caused them to compete with each other for the same programming time. Essentially, homework help has different goals than tutoring, which has different goals than enrichment or other program curricula, and distinctions among the purposes as well as time given to each was viewed as critical by these interviewees. Without a developed, distinct intention, the time becomes less productive (S. Piha, personal communication, January 10, 2001; M. Yoders, personal communication, August 16, 2001).

A final challenge consistently cited by programs was a lack of resources. Desired resources could be as simple as needing copies of students' school-day textbooks or wanting materials such as games, activity books, or curriculum kits for those children who finish before their peers. Unevenness in resources among programs was apparent when one program simply wanted computers, while another wanted Internet access, and a third wanted training for staff in the use of both. It would seem that without the resources to provide all three programs feel unable to give children access to the kind of technology that so many of them lack at home and that is a given in middle-class homes. Furthermore, two programs specifically mentioned their inability to pay competitive salaries as a major roadblock to offering better homework support; as one director put it, "You get what you pay for." They implied that better compensation might attract more qualified staff members, who have more knowledge and skill on which to base the homework help they give. This issue becomes especially important as school learning content becomes increasingly challenging, even for adults. Finally, programs cited a lack of time and space for children to work off school-day tensions. One program director noted that currently the children in his program get no time to play outside at all. Without appropriate space and time for children to relax in before setting out to complete homework, misbehavior and distractibility tend to become more of an issue than they need to be. Misbehavior can detract from the amount of quality work both the misbehaving child and any other children present would get done, due to its intrinsically distracting and disruptive nature. Thus, the resources programs need to provide effective homework programming are varied, and some of the needs will be easier to meet than others.

Recommendations

Some recommendations will aid programs in their homework practices, no matter which of the three orientations toward homework characterizes them. For instance, the literature on homework recommends providing children with a consistent and specific place and time to complete homework (Amundson, 1995; Hong & Milgram, 2000; Marzano, 2001; Paulu, 1995) and points out that homework is best accomplished with a student-to-staff ratio of less than 10:1 (O'Connor & McGuire, 1998; R. Weinstein, personal communication, August 8, 2001). Many of the programs we interviewed utilized volunteer tutors to reduce the student to staff ratio further than this, and from all accounts a smaller ratio created more successful homework practices, though more research is needed to confirm this impression.

Such practices take on the quality of rituals in many programs and ideally incorporate clear transitions between the end of school and the beginning of afterschool, allowing children to feel that they have entered a separate culture where their problems in school do not have to follow them. Interestingly, two programs felt that at least a half hour of free time (distinct from snack time) before embarking upon any other activities made for an invaluable improvement to the efficacy of homework and other program curricular activities (M. Duke, personal communication, October 18, 2001; C. Swalay, personal communication, October 10, 2001).

Dedicated Space

Space for homework activities is also an important factor to think about when structuring homework time. Space is a factor not often under the control of the program, but whenever possible children and staff should be given an opportunity to personalize homework space. In addition, a number of different environments for completing homework according to different learning styles is ideal: single desks, tables for groups, a "cozy" corner; homework space should be designed to give children choices similar to those available in the home. Perhaps most important, however, is that children be given choices as to what sorts of spaces in which to do their homework, and that formal and informal spaces be made available to accommodate both individual workers and small groups (Hong & Milgram, 2000; WFD, 2000). Schools, libraries, and universities need to be encouraged to share their space during off hours and allow programs greater autonomy while occupying that space, and to give programs access to adequate storage in between sessions. As a field we need to get beyond the "school cafeteria approach" to homework. These large spaces can make young people feel anonymous. If they must be used, personalizing will go a long way toward creating an atmosphere more conducive to homework.

Time

The amount of time a child should spend on homework is a topic that generates many opinions. Of course, how much homework time is needed in a program depends in large part on the grade level of participating students. The National Parent Teacher Association (NPTA) and National Education Association (NEA) recommend ten to 20 minutes of homework for kindergarten to second-grade students and 30 to 60 minutes for third- to sixth-grade students (NPTA, 2000). Cooper calls this the "ten-minute rule," where the optimum amount of time spent on homework is the child's grade multiplied by ten minutes (Cooper, 2001b, p. 37). A U.S. Department of Education publication suggests that even less homework is optimal for younger children and more for older children, recommending no more than 20 minutes for first to third grades, 20 to 40 minutes for fourth through sixth grades, and up to two hours for seventh through ninth grades (Paulu, 1995). Harris Cooper has advised that students in first through third grades spend ten to 45 minutes on homework, fourth through sixth grades 45 to 90 minutes, and seventh through ninth grades 60 to 90 minutes (Cooper, 1989, cited in Cooper, 2001a). While teachers and schools may or may not follow these guidelines, afterschool programs can and should when looking to schedule homework into their day. Based on the studies above, 30 minutes of homework time for children in the third grade or below and 60 minutes for children in the sixth grade or below should provide enough time to finish or make significant progress toward finishing a day's assignments. No matter how much homework children get, spending more time than is developmentally appropriate in one sitting is likely to frustrate a child's attention and motivation and yields no proven benefits (Cooper, 2001a). The rationale for spending certain amounts of time on homework did not relate to developmentally appropriate standards, but instead followed a "one size fits all" approach. We recommend that programs consider carefully how much homework time is appropriate for their youth, and also that programs provide older children with more homework time without requiring younger children to participate longer than developmentally appropriate.

Giving Feedback

Of course, the fact that some children may be forced to rush or struggle to finish their homework in the allotted time creates a challenge, especially when parents expect their children to arrive home with their homework done. If children in a program regularly experience difficulty with homework assignments, or cannot complete them in a developmentally appropriate span of time, or both, programs can do the child a tremendous service by passing that information on to both parents and teachers. Ideally, this information sharing would begin a dialogue among children's caregivers (parents, school teachers, afterschool personnel) about the purposes of homework and how struggling students might be supported by all three types of caregivers, through teachers modifying assignments, parents providing additional dedicated homework time, and programs recruiting tutors for more concentrated one-on-one help.

As afterschool programs organize and create sophisticated networks incorporating parents and school staff, they will become more able to provide excellent feedback not only to individual teachers or schools, but also to district school departments to assist with homework practices and policies. The stronger the connection between program staff and schools, the more useful such feedback will be. The positive potential here for afterschool programs individually or collectively is immense. Indeed, programs and staff can help give a voice to parents, who often feel isolated or disempowered in relation to the educational process.

Changing Staff Attitudes

Changing staff attitudes toward homework may be a goal for programs where homework time has been unproductive or viewed mainly as an imposition. To inspire staff buy-in, knowing and agreeing to the goals of homework time is an important first step. Staff must be given a way to see that homework doesn't have to be an imposition, but instead can facilitate more creative programming. For one thing, homework gives staff an indication of where their youth are "at" in their school studies: topics and skills on which their teachers seem to be focusing and students' attitude toward their studies. This information can be useful for planning and structuring other learning activities, field trips, and so forth. At one community art center we visited, the director had instituted a "case load" approach whereby her staff was assigned a particular group of students during homework help time for several weeks. By working with the same students over time, the staff gained a deeper understanding of the students' academic needs and could provide more tailored interventions. Doing homework doesn't have to mean that time spent will be dull or uninspiring. Staff should be given a say and a role in creating homework practices and goals for the program. Thus, homework can contribute meaningfully toward making afterschool feel different and creating a sense of ownership and teamwork among staff.

A serious challenge to staff buy-in, however, is that of providing discussions, training, and support for staff to accomplish the program's homework goals. For a staff made up of school-day teachers, support has to include help in making even the homework part of afterschool feel different from the school day. Teachers need help creating and maintaining a different atmosphere during afterschool, especially if they are working in their regular classrooms and/or with their usual students. On the other hand, staff who are youth development workers may need extra help in seeing the place and benefit of homework in afterschool. Homework help is rarely the type of work professionals in the youth development field look forward to doing. For these workers, it must be made clear that homework is one important way to support academic achievement, but that it can and should be balanced with physical, emotional, and social needs, as well as other types of intentional learning (O'Connor & McGuire, 1998). For most afterschool professionals, the real heart of afterschool programs is the "other" learning goals, which can include arts, technology, science, literacy, math, projects, sports, and any number of other activities that encourage children to learn about and engage in the world around them in meaningful ways.

In both types of staffing situations, creating a collaborative environment where staff are encouraged to share their ideas, challenges, and successes through regular meetings is a key to success. The point here is not just to train staff, but to engage them in the creation of time and space that is both different from school and supportive of learning. Of course, the biggest challenge for any program is finding the time and money to sustain such ongoing support and collaboration. This points toward an important gap that outside funders or technical service providers might be able to fill.

Training

Staff and volunteers will need to know how to deal with assisting students individually and in small groups, helping students organize their assignments, motivating reluctant and frustrated students, and handling behavioral problems. Training should provide staff and volunteers with clear distinctions between the goals and practices of homework and those of tutoring. Some knowledge of the content and methods of instruction being used in schools is also vital. Andria Fletcher of the Center for Collaborative

Solutions argued for this type of training because staff, even undergraduate volunteers, have been out of the school system for a number of years, and teaching methods often change dramatically in short periods of time, particularly in math (personal communication, October 24, 2001). In fact, she had seen cases where children had done worse on their assignments as a result of the help because it was not consonant with current methods.

One program where we interviewed came up with a unique solution to the academic content portion of homework training, namely, providing volunteers with a resource binder that included information about topics and standards for the children served. These undergraduate volunteers also received training updates on a weekly basis. This program was based in a school and was staffed by classroom teachers along with dozens of college volunteers. Despite the participation of school-day teachers in the after-school program, getting access to teachers' curricula proved challenging even for this program, making the binders less specific than they might have been about learning topics and goals for the children. Another difficulty this program faced was promoting greater collaboration and partnership between the teachers and volunteers. It might be helpful in the future to conduct a half-day retreat for teachers and students, allowing them to interact informally and develop common goals.

Internet Resources

A further recommendation for programs looking to offer specialized assistance in difficult academic subjects is to seek out Internet help options. Recently, websites staffed by schoolteachers, undergraduate students, and even university professors have sprung up on the Internet. Locally, Harvard University undergraduates collaborated with the Boston Public Library (BPL) system to offer online homework help; this service, called Harvard Online Tutoring, is available through any BPL branch office and primarily serves high school students. Such services are low-fuss, no-cost options of which programs and their youth may avail themselves.

Research

Given the dearth of research on homework in afterschool program contexts, we strongly recommend research into the comparative effectiveness of different homework practices on both program atmosphere and academic achievement research and partnership directions. The topic is too important to leave to unquestioned confidence in the efficacy of specific practices or even homework itself. Programs implementing changes in their homework practices could provide insight into how different practices generate different attitudes and outcomes in staff and youth. Basic research in this area is underway with Policy Studies Associates and The After-School Corporation in New York City. They have looked at the efficacy of language arts and math homework help in terms of various achievement indicators. In initial analyses, homework help in math was shown to improve the academic achievement of low-performing students (E. Reisner, personal communication, October, 25, 2001). The next step will be to confirm these results and explore the actual techniques being utilized to elucidate why homework help in math might be more efficacious than help in language arts.

Connecting Enriched Curricula with Schools

Given the fact that homework is the most common example of extended learning found in afterschool, and also the fact that homework typically makes students, parents, and afterschool staff the passive recipients of learning mandates, we recommend enriching homework content as a way of making the experience more meaningful and rewarding.

Rather than simply helping children to perform homework assignments, afterschool staff should be empowered to develop enriched curricular activities that meet the same learning goals as homework. For example, creative learning exploration using a science kit tied to the school curriculum could substitute for certain kinds of science homework. We feel that children would be much more eager to engage in such activities than in completing worksheet-type homework assignments. Naturally, the use of enriched curricula to fulfill homework requirements would require a close and open collaboration between schools and afterschool programs in order to evaluate the productivity of different kinds of assignments and to refine the curricula as necessary. Such collaboration could take the form of committees set up by schools and afterschool programs to devise new homework practices that support and build on the strengths of afterschool settings. Homework could thereby become increasingly project oriented, with a strong focus on community involvement, acknowledging the fact that children and youth typically work in groups. For their part, afterschool programs could make use of projects and enriched curricula to forge stronger and more complex connections to communities. The Citizen Schools are excellent examples of afterschool programs building on the rich expertise of Boston's communities. With the proper support, training, and scholarly inquiry, homework can stop representing an unwelcome infiltration of afterschool time by the school day, and become a tool for building relationships, improving academic skills, and discovering new ways of conceptualizing and engaging in learning.

However, we do not wish to lose sight of the fact that afterschool programs now serve as a great equalizer for students whose parents are not in a position to help them with their homework, such as immigrant families with a lack of English proficiency (M. Suárez-Orozco, personal communication, February 28, 2002). One young person we discussed this issue with told us the afterschool program helped with homework and "my grades went up. I never connected homework with doing better in school. It seems too simple, but it never occurred to me!" (Youth panel, Gear Up afterschool program at the Cleveland Grove Middle School, May 2001).

Chapter 3

Enriched Afterschool Learning

The Role of Curricula

Chapter Overview

In this chapter we review the nature and importance of learning in afterschool. After addressing this topic, we discuss patterns of curricular practices found in our research. We then summarize the challenges cited by interviewees, and conclude by offering a series of recommendations for effecting better enriched learning in afterschool programs.

Why Enriched Learning Curricula in Afterschool?

While learning has often been dichotomized as formal or informal by curricula theorists, learning as it occurs in afterschool programs shares characteristics of both. According to Scribner and Cole (1973), formal education is deliberate and routine, covers generally valued skills or qualities, and takes place in specialized environments, whereas informal education is more serendipitous and participatory, involves empathizing and identifying with teachers, and can take place anywhere. In many ways the contrast between these two types of education mirrors the differences found in teaching and learning experiences in home and school environments.

Although both formal and informal learning can occur in schools, the union of the two seems particularly natural to afterschool settings. As discussed in earlier chapters, afterschool programs function as intermediary spaces in children's lives, and it is this positioning of afterschool that makes the mingling of formal and informal education intrinsic to it.

When asked what learning in afterschool settings should look like, our interviewees most commonly described the dual nature of afterschool learning in this way: "Learning in afterschool programs should be *connected to* but *distinctive from* the regular school day." Beyond this widespread description, we found that the interviewees' professional roles as a direct-service practitioner, policymaker, or researcher tended to influence the details of their answers. Practitioners tended to answer in terms of practices (e.g., they were oriented toward results and had numeracy and literacy focuses), whereas respondents who were not direct-service providers were often more concerned with issues of program culture (e.g., student support and choices) or political imperatives (e.g., the relation to school standards). At the same time, some general themes emerged consistently, suggesting the presence of a shared vision in the field of the distinctive character and goals of learning in afterschool:

1. Learning should be experiential, focused on relevant, exploratory, and hands-on experiences.
2. Learning should center upon engaging, fascinating topics that capture children's imaginations.
3. Learning should be multimodal, offering multiple "points of entry" and means of reinforcement. We found a strong identification among our interviewees with Multiple Intelligences theory (Gardner, 1999).
4. Learning should be holistic, acknowledging each child's developmental needs along several axes: cognitive, physical, moral, spiritual, emotional, and social.
5. Learning should be concerned with basic skill development, especially literacy and numeracy skills that reinforce school learning, and teaching "soft" skills related to school and job readiness.

It is perhaps unsurprising that learning as it was described by our interviewees echoes the visions for education espoused by many key theorists in the education field. For instance, Dewey (1916) argued strenuously for each of the first four points throughout his career. More recently, Gardner (1991) has emphasized that, to promote true understanding rather than rote learning, educational efforts must utilize multiple modalities, connect evidently and meaningfully to students' lives, and promote synthesis. Ball and Heath (1993) argue that, in addition to development of basic skills, children require opportunities to develop "soft" skills, and that this learning is best fostered not through a didactic approach, but through an experiential one. Children not only develop organizational and problem-solving skills more readily when faced with motivating and authentic experiences that require these skills, they also reinforce their understanding of basic skills, such as literacy and numeracy, by utilizing them in authentic ways (Gardner, 1991; Katz & Chard, 2000). An experiential approach promotes children's development of social, physical, and other skills in tandem with skills more closely aligned to academics.

The incorporation of both formal and informal learning experiences in afterschool programs is closely tied to its voluntary nature. Because youth can choose not to attend, afterschool programs must work to make any educational undertaking engaging and fun for youth. Working to connect learning to children's experiences and interests is the main way that programs try to arouse and maintain interest. Prioritizing engagement gives programs the opportunity to build children's intrinsic motivation to learn (Katz & Chard, 2000; Larson, 2000). The voluntary nature of participation also requires more authentic and collaborative learning and more informal relationships with adults, all of which contribute to giving children a greater sense of ownership of their own learning, thus reinforcing the motivation to learn (Heath, 1992).

While the vision put forth above is undoubtedly idealistic, it provides a powerful set of principles around which to organize enrichment activities in afterschool, be they explicitly academic or primarily recreational. When these elements are brought together, the learning becomes fun and is often able to break through the anxiety, resistance, or exasperation children can feel when confronted with learning tasks after a full day of school. This notion of embedding learning in fun so that children are learning without realizing it was articulated by Andria Fletcher, an After School Intermediary with the Center for Collaborative Solutions, as "disguised learning" (A. Fletcher, personal communication, October 24, 2001). Kristen Pineo, education director of the West End House Boys and Girls Club, echoed the same idea when she described how most of her program's activities incorporated a "secret learning piece" (K. Pineo, personal communication, October 15, 2001). Such descriptions of learning were offered in nearly all of our interviews. Thus, the challenge for afterschool practitioners is to create programming that combines learning and fun as twin and equal aims. Below we describe some of the curricular options available to programs as they take on this challenge.

Curricular Options

A number of curricular options are available to programs looking to incorporate educational enrichment that meets the above criteria into their schedules. While limitations of space prevent us from trying to describe and assess all the curricula available to afterschool staff, it is possible to sketch out a typology of approaches, providing examples for each type:

- prepackaged curricula
- scaffold curricula
- activity-based curricula
- project-based curricula

In developing our typology, we found it useful to conceptualize curricular options according to the amount of structure and content they offered relative to other existing options (see Figure 1).

Our research revealed that, while some practitioners may have a philosophical affinity or aversion toward a particular type of curriculum, as yet there exists no evidence that one type is necessarily better than another. Each has strengths and drawbacks that make it more or less suitable, depending on staff and program characteristics and needs as well as educational goals. Choosing a curriculum, then, is a matter of proclivity, goals,

FIGURE 1   *A Typology of Afterschool Curricular Options Delineating the Relative Amounts of Structure and Content They Offer*

Predefined Content

		High	Low
Structure	High	Prepackaged	Scaffold
	Low	Activity-based	Project-based

and fit. Furthermore, our typology should not be construed as outlining mutually exclusive categories; clearly, some enrichment activities will combine elements from more than one type.[1]

Prepackaged Curricula

"Prepackaged" curricula offer both content and structure. They offer structure through a set sequence of activities and content through teacher or staff manuals, lesson plans, and materials, all available for purchase. Typically, they offer a complete educational package for a set amount of time, ranging from a month to a year. They are typically focused on academic standards, especially on literacy and numeracy skills. Because the curricula are created for a large national audience, the standards drawn upon tend to be from the state or national level. While spontaneous discussion and freer activities may occur during implementation of the curriculum, the timing, topics, and goals of activities tend to be predetermined.

A number of programs use school-based curricula, such as *Tribal Rhythms* (Cooperative Artists Institute, 2000), and adapt them to the afterschool context. Some curricula, however, are designed specifically for afterschool programs, such as *Foundations Travels* (Clement, Lauer, & Wolhafe, 2000), *KidzLit* (Developmental Studies Center, 2000), and the *Design It!*

1.   We do not endorse any of the specific curricula we cite in illustrating the types of curricula now available.

curriculum developed by the Boston Children's Museum and the Boston Museum of Science in partnership with the Education Development Center (EDC), the National Institute for Out-of-School Time (NIOST), and other research and museum partners.

The *Design It!* curriculum gives afterschool staff a thorough understanding of how to implement it (T. Porter, personal communication, September 19, 2001). The curriculum offers multiple design activities on an engineering topic for weeks of programming. The approach is cooperative and kinesthetic, allowing children to learn about engineering and design, which are included in Massachusetts state standards, in a manner that does not replicate school work. The museum staff takes the curriculum to sites, trains program staff in its implementation, provides a kit with requisite materials, and provides ongoing support. New parts of the curriculum are shared with programs through a monthly workshop, where the museum's staff models implementation for program staff. A member from the museum's staff also visits sites at least monthly to help with on-site implementation. Thus far, the curricula have been piloted with five Boston and Cambridge programs and will be expanded to five more programs next year.

In contrast to the *Design It!* engineering curriculum are curricula that center on literature, such as the three K–6 curricula published by Foundations, Inc.: *Foundations Travels, Foundations Discovers,* and *Foundations Invents.* The themes of the Foundations curricula are further divided into units focused on such topics as civic and global responsibility, creative expression, and technology. The curricula are literature-based, interdisciplinary investigations, based on national standards in English and math. A program purchasing a Foundations curriculum would receive a comprehensive teacher's manual with lessons for a yearlong program, and a book list (a class pack of books is also available for purchase). The manual is designed to be "structured and yet flexible" (Foundations, 2000). Interestingly, in our research of program practices in Harvard's host communities, a few programs had adapted school curricula, but almost no one used afterschool-specific curricula.

Programs looking for a complete, "teacher-proof" package that requires little training in its usage may look to prepackaged curricula. Laura Wolhafe, education director at Foundations, Inc., mentioned two general categories of programs that tend to make use of the Foundations curricula (L. Wolhafe, personal communication, October 19, 2001). There are programs that have just gotten a grant, and other programs that are under pressure to improve their educational component. We observed this curriculum in spring 2001 at a Children's Aid Society school in Washington Heights, a primarily Latino neighborhood in New York City where Spanish was the first language of most residents and their children. The director said that the program had had a great deal of trouble with the educational component required by its funding agent because her staff were not trained in curriculum design and instruction. When she bought the curriculum, the afterschool teachers began to feel a new sense of competence and professionalism; they had lesson plans and engaging activity units. The educational aspect of the program literally improved overnight.

Clearly, prepackaged curricula have their benefits and can accommodate a certain amount of flexibility. In some situations, especially those in which afterschool practitioners do not have much formal education, skills, or training, prepackaged curricula can be a very useful solution. Such curricula can also be beneficial to programs with high turnover in that, as practitioners leave and are hired, the content of the program maintains continuity. One drawback of such curricula, though, is that they might be regarded as taking control away from the afterschool staff, an already undervalued group. Furthermore, the creators of some curricula, such as the *Design It!* curriculum, stress that successful implementation of such curricula requires a solid program infrastructure and commitment. Also, scripted lessons leave less room for learning in afterschool to be responsive to the evolving needs and interests of children and staff. Finally, these curricula often cannot be reused from year to year because the children will have already seen the material, making for an annual expense.

Scaffold Curricula

Another type of curriculum available to programs is what we call "scaffold" curriculum. Scaffold curricula are different from prepackaged curricula in that they offer a general framework into which activities chosen by the program and its practitioners can be fit. In other words, they offer structure but not content, much as a scaffold is a structural support to a building or an outline is an organizational guide to an essay. Learning goals are not achieved by specifying activities, but by providing a framework to organize activities. Program staff develop a schedule of program offerings within this structure.

One example of this kind of curriculum is the Boys and Girls Clubs of America's (BGCA) comprehensive enrichment strategy called *Project Learn*. *Project Learn* is founded on Reginald Clark's research (1992), which indicates that disadvantaged students succeed when they engage in "high-yield learning activities" during their out-of-school time. BGCA used this study to specify that, as part of *Project Learn*, every club should offer members approximately 25 to 35 hours per week of high-yield learning activities, organized by category (e.g., leisure reading: four to five hours; writing activities: one to two hours; and discussions with knowledgeable adults: four to five hours. Staff members are free to develop a specific program of activities, based on these guidelines, according to the local culture and strengths of each Club.

One important advantage of this approach is that it provides staff with an overall idea for how to structure programming, but also allows them room to explore topics of interest to them and the program youth, which may not overlap with topics presented in more structured curricula. The drawback here is that a curriculum of this sort requires staff to spend a great deal of time planning and coordinating their efforts. Thus, training and regular staff meetings become important when a program decides to utilize this sort of curriculum; otherwise it could be overwhelming or ineffective.

Activity-Based Curricula

"Activity-based" curricula are quite different from scaffold curricula. Rather than offering an overall structure for a program with no content, nearly the opposite is true. An activity-based curriculum consists primarily of materials for hands-on activities. There may also be a resource guide to support staff in implementation and organizational issues, or supplemental trainings, but they do not tend to have the elaborate sequencing and scripting components of prepackaged curriculum. Activity-based curricula are further distinguished from prepackaged curricula by their strong focus on generating products.

These curricula often articulate exploratory and constructivist learning principles by offering a set of elemental pieces (discovery objects, construction units), which may be assembled and used according to the aims of the participants. *Lego®* offers some clear examples of this type. Other activity-based curricula have a narrow product objective, such as a model-building set. An unusual example of such an activity-based curriculum is *Lucy, the Inflatable Whale* (WhaleNet, 2001). The objective of this curriculum is to construct a life-size whale so that children can appreciate the size of humpback whales while engaging in a fun group effort. In either case, activity curricula can be described as "modular" because they easily function to reinforce a larger unit through a supplemental hands-on experience or to constitute a self-contained module.

The Academy of Engineering Labs (PCS Edventures.COM, 2002) produces an activity-based curriculum with some strong prepackaged curricular elements. Materials for engineering projects, machine-building, and *Lego®* construction are available for purchase. In addition, the vendor provides technical assistance, class outlines, and online assessment tools. This level of support, however, is unusual for activity-based curricula. More common are activity kits, like the ones provided by museums. Museum kits generally come with a supply of materials and books that can be used to investigate a topic, along with curriculum and resource binders that include implementation suggestions. Training is often available separately.

In Boston, the Children's Museum, Museum of Science, and New England Aquarium each offer kits, ranging from a single activity-based exploration to a full two-week curriculum.[2] Smaller kits touch on a variety of topics that might be covered in one or two days, such as the Children's Museum kits on cultural celebrations (e.g., Cambodian New Year, Kwanzaa, and Têt) or the New England Aquarium kits on specific animals (e.g., otters, penguins, and manatee). An example of a kit that might take about a week to fully implement is the Children's Museum kit called *Ghana Today*. The *Ghana Today* kit contains a video, photos, a large number of books,

---

2. Boston museums are at the forefront of museum-based education, offering a multitude of low-cost services and materials to schools and afterschool staff and children. The generosity of Joel Rubin of the New England Aquarium and Juli Brownrigg and Tim Porter of The Children's Museum was essential to our understanding of the curricular options they offer.

and a variety of artifacts, such as a flag, a child's school uniform, money, and cloth, all from Ghana. The teacher's guide that comes with this kit gives suggestions for which books are appropriate for children from kindergarten through fifth grade, as well as ways to explore the video, photos, and artifacts with children, and it links these activities to the Massachusetts Curriculum Frameworks. Examples of larger kits are the Children's Museum Ancient China kit, the New England Aquarium Whales kit, and the Museum of Science Electricity kit. These kits offer a great array of activity options.

Clearly, the modularity and adaptability of activity-based curricula are their main advantage. Also, children enjoy their hands-on nature, which provides natural opportunities for cooperative learning and problem-solving. The challenge in implementing these curricula is that they require staff with either a great deal of knowledge on a topic or at least with the time to access supports (and in some cases, training) offered by the producers of the curricula. We learned from the Children's Museum and New England Aquarium representatives that afterschool programs generally do not take advantage of kits or trainings, largely due to lack of funding and time (J. Rubin, personal communication, August 30, 2001; J. Brownrigg, personal communication, September 19, 2001). Thus to make these curricula more appealing and effective for afterschool use, museums may need to develop alternative supports for afterschool programs, such as web-based discussions and question-and-answer environments. The Children's Museum has made strides in this direction by designing afterschool materials called CATS (Curriculum Arts Technology and Science) kits. These kits are being piloted in five afterschool programs in Boston and surrounding suburbs, and there are plans to focus on broadening the pilot to Boston Community Centers in the near future. An integral part of this initiative is a half-day training session. This initiative will be an important one to learn from in terms of both challenges and the supports that help overcome them when implementing activity-based curricula.

Project-Based Learning

Project-based learning is less a type of curriculum that can be classified according to structure and content as an approach to teaching and learning that emphasizes collaboration and group determination.[3] Project-based learning is founded on the theory that children should learn through sustained engagement with a topic of interest to a group (and import to the community), which yields some product or performable skill. Thus, project-based learning is distinguished from other curricular options by its democratic and self-generated nature. The details of this approach will be discussed more below. It is worth noting here, however, that we found almost no programs in Boston or Cambridge, Massachusetts, that engaged in project-based learning in the way we will describe. Many considered themselves to be doing "projects" defined usually as "product-oriented activity," but the components of sustained engagement, meaningful output, and child-centeredness were often lacking.

Four main elements guide project-based learning: participation, fun, learning, and products that matter. This approach to projects was generated in a collaboration among Harvard Project Zero (PZ), the Program in After-school Education and Research at Harvard (PAER), and The After-School Corporation (TASC). Program staff members are charged with developing deep understanding and engagement in children and youth by evaluating their curriculum at every step against these goals. For example, when deciding on a topic, staff members should ask themselves: Is this going to be fun for the youth? Is it relevant and important to them? Can we incorporate fun opportunities like field trips and performances? What learning goals can be articulated around this topic, especially related to statewide standards? What products or skills will result from the exploration that can be shared with others? Many projects will end in a service activity, such as donating the proceeds of a performance to charity, as participants attempt to make their learning visible and meaningful to the larger community. In general, practitioners emphasize the importance of working in small, cooperative groups to facilitate relationship-building, and providing continuous opportunities for students to make decisions. Over the past two-and-a-half years this collaborative group developed a training and implementation

3. Our discussion of project-based learning was informed considerably by an interview with Steve Seidel and Tina Blythe of Harvard Project Zero (personal communication, October 10, 2001), and by our joint project-based work with The After-School Corporation in New York City.

guide (*Fun Learning Matters*), and conducted workshops and ongoing site-based consultation.

In a project-based learning program we developed for fifth-grade students in New York City, group leaders developed some general goals for the project during the planning phase, such as "students will create crafts available for sale" and "they will learn how to realistically price items they will sell" (Blythe, Boyd, Wilson, & Noam, 2002). These goals were shared with the children, who then as a group created a more specific outline of the project. Based on their concerns and the materials at their disposal, the children decided to make and sell jewelry boxes and donate the proceeds to the American Cancer Society. The group leaders guided the students through all of the intermediary steps toward this goal, including the math lessons required to price merchandise and calculate profit. In the end, the children had the satisfaction of presenting an oversized check to the American Cancer Society at a PTA meeting in front of family and teachers.

The guiding principles of project-based learning are notably similar to those of afterschool learning as defined by our interviewees, making it a natural option for programs looking to maximize what is considered best about afterschool learning. As with activity-based curricula, the exhibition component provides the staff a ready means of evaluating what youth have learned without needing to test their knowledge. The exhibition can also be an occasion to bring together parents, community members, and school personnel in a celebratory spirit, highlighting the important work of the afterschool program and providing an opportunity for sharing information. In the case of the "donating dollars" exhibition, the community included extended families with alarming numbers of cancer cases and the association that leads the fight against this illness. The major challenge of project-based learning is that it requires extensive planning time, access to materials, and, possibly, off-site locations for field trips. Since the instructor's role is that of a facilitator, more sophisticated teaching skills are required than in any other curriculum type. In addition, we have found that project-based learning requires breaking down many large tasks into smaller steps, a process that requires initial trainings and ongoing coaching.

Challenges

One of the main challenges staff face in developing a successful educational enrichment component is simply the range and variety of curricular options that are available. In this section we have focused on curricula that can be purchased or formally classified across programs, rather than on the innumerable ways that practitioners provide enrichment activities. Several programs where we interviewed, for example, used games or discussion groups to stimulate learning through nontraditional methods. Many programs offer workshops or mini-courses on innovative topics as part of their enrichment component. All of this variation is further complicated by the fact that there are no easy criteria for matching a curriculum to program goals. The variables that must be considered (and are often hard to predict for the life of the curriculum) are cost, youth characteristics, staff competencies, appropriateness of themes, supports and technical assistance resources, program storage capacity (long- and short-term), adaptability, and longevity of the curriculum. Programs must also consider what kinds of outcome data they might need to report and whether the curriculum lends itself to that sort of assessment.

The cost of enrichment curricula is a factor worthy of some attention, since the purchasable curricula mentioned in this section range in price from several hundred dollars to about $20 thousand. Programs operating on a small budget may find this cost prohibitive. The unfortunate resulting paradox has been summed up by Dr. Pilar O'Cadiz from the Collaborative After School Project in California: "Prepackaged curricula can be helpful to programs that lack personnel trained in educational program design. However they are often costly and hence not available to those very programs that are not well staffed in the first place" (P. O'Cadiz, personal communication, August 14, 2001). When training is available in the use of a curriculum, programs may be unwilling to pay for staff members to attend because the high attrition rate in the school-age care profession makes the impact of such investments potentially short lived.

The museum staff we interviewed identified staff member turnover as a major roadblock. This issue is seen as a challenge to choosing and implementing curricula because training has to start over again when staff members leave. Even when the curriculum is an activity-based one, arguably requiring less training because of its modularity, once the staff persons who knew how to access the museums' kits leave, the knowledge of that resource leaves with them. As one museum staff member put it, programs facing these challenges can have short "memories," making training a repetitive and expensive process (J. Brownrigg, personal communication, September 19, 2001).

Given the diversity of experience that afterschool staff members bring along with them to programs, the choice of which type of curriculum is most suitable can be a difficult one. When a program's staff has a wide variety of experience and skills, a curricular option that is perfect for one staff member may be too restrictive or too unstructured for another. Furthermore, the curricular option that fits a program's staff today may not be such a good fit tomorrow.

Many programs face a tension between allocating resources and time to enrichment activities versus homework or free play. Several program directors articulated this tension as the difficult balancing act between academic and social learning, or rigor and relaxation. While enrichment is central to the role played by afterschool programs in the lives of children, it is often not recognized or esteemed by outsiders. One program director who assured enriched learning for youth recalled a parent storming into her office because her child had not completed his homework during the afterschool program. How programs balance these pressures, opportunities, and obligations plays a critical role in whether they will be seen as successful or ineffectual.

Recommendations

In general, more research-based curricula specifically formulated for afterschool settings are needed. Too often programs are forced to buy an entire package curriculum developed for the school even though most of it will have to be adapted or discarded because of the particular constraints of the nonschool context. Curricula should be rigorously evaluated by vendors and should come with suggested assessments whenever possible, thereby easing some of the burden of adaptation for programs. Furthermore, universities and other organizations must take up the task of conducting evaluation studies and long-term research that compare outcomes (e.g., academic, social, and psychological) of different curricular approaches. Studies that look at the effectiveness of particular types of curricula with certain child and youth populations are also greatly needed. Such studies could yield techniques that providers might find useful in adapting curricula to children's needs in the same way that Lisa Delpit's (1995) work has helped literacy teachers modify their instruction for black and minority children.

Our other recommendations will focus on two areas that have wide application: training and building infrastructure, and incorporating positive youth development goals.

Training and Supplementary Curricula

We cannot overstate the importance of training in the effective, developmentally appropriate implementation of any curriculum, particularly project-based learning where practitioners may literally be starting from scratch. As Tina Blythe and Steve Seidel of Project Zero explained, one of the largest mistakes made by those attempting to execute project-based learning is to take on too big a project with the first try (T. Blythe and S. Seidel, personal communication, October 10, 2001). Furthermore, there tends to be the assumption that a staff committed to project-based learning should have projects lined up back-to-back, but Tina Blythe asserted that such a model is exhausting not only for staff, but also for children. Thus, even if a program has chosen project-based learning as its main curriculum, it must also have a supplementary curriculum for use between projects. To understand these complexities, training that incorporates examples of feasible projects and implementation tips is invaluable in making such a curricular choice a successful one. It will become important to provide sample projects to programs that are flexible, yet offer staff structure. In the PAER/ PZ /TASC collaboration, for example, the next phase of work will include making learning goals explicit, practicing skills needed to create projects, and possibly tying projects to explicit academic goals.

Education Specialists

Because the need for these trainings is as universal and persistent for after-school staff as it is for classroom teachers who receive regular professional development throughout the year, we propose that community-wide Education Specialists (ES) be trained and hired to support the learning goals of clusters of programs. Education Specialists would be knowledgeable about statewide standards and curriculum for each grade level, and they would have experience in progressive teaching methods. They would provide the support programs need to develop logic models for their learning content so that learning goals are articulated, connected to school-related competencies, and tied explicitly to enrichment activities. The very presence of the ES would likely spur programs to articulate their learning objectives and reconsider the fit between their methods and goals even if they have not done this in the past.

The ES or another representative from an intermediary organization should also take on some of the responsibility for being a knowledge and resource broker between schools and afterschool programs. At the community level, schools must make a commitment to support the educational enrichment activities of the afterschool programs that serve their students. After all, the success of those efforts will contribute to the success of the school's educational mission. Locally, the Boston and Cambridge Public School Boards should consider ways that their curriculum could be enhanced through certain projects or children's exposure to a particular prepackaged or activity-based curriculum. Boston Public Schools has begun this process by hosting a training session called Bridging the Gap that oriented afterschool staff to the district's approach to instruction, and suggested ways it could be reinforced during out-of-school time. This sharing of information should occur as a give-and-take, motivated by the recognition that both parties gain when the channels of communication are opened, rather than as an invitation to schools to usurp the enrichment components of afterschool programs. Many school officials have begun to educate themselves about the unique possibilities of afterschool and become partners in supporting its development. Most of the programs where we interviewed welcome the opportunity to collaborate with schools on this ambitious agenda.

Including Private Schools

Private schools, with their rich resources and long experience with project-based learning, could serve as ideal partners in developing enriched curricula and projects for afterschool time. In essence, the qualities that we aspire to infuse into afterschool learning thrive in many private school classrooms. Private school faculties should be invited to run workshops, attend conferences with other afterschool practitioners, and participate in the exchange of ideas and techniques around enriched learning. Summerbridge, a national program that focuses on academic enrichment, has already identified private schools as powerful partners. At Providence Summerbridge, for example, the program directors are members of the private school's faculty and operate the program on the premises. During the summer session, teachers from the school serve as curriculum coaches.

Youth Empowerment

The child-centered nature of learning in afterschool programs is one of the features that distinguishes it from school-day learning, where much of the curriculum is predetermined by the state. As such, we recommend that the students' interests and choices be incorporated into the content of enriched learning to the greatest extent possible. Giving students choices builds their decisionmaking skills and sense of agency. As children enter adolescence, this measure of autonomy is critical for their development (Eccles, 1999). Voice and choice also deepen students' engagement with a subject as they see how particular skills help them achieve a desired goal. In the end we hope that these students will grow to see themselves as learners actively constructing knowledge in the world.

While each group of students will be different, some research has been done about what youth tend to want from afterschool programs. In a highly informative report called "After-School Programs in Boston: What young people think and want," Lindsay, Pollack, and their colleagues (2002) present results from focus groups with Boston children and teens. Youth generally describe wanting afterschool programs that support all aspects of their development while being safe, nurturing, accessible, and physically appropriate to the needs of the program. In terms of learning, youth showed a preference for experiential ("hands-on") learning that leads to new products or skills. They also wanted relevant learning experiences, such as discussions about sex or college field trips, that would benefit them personally and professionally. Finally, students asserted the importance of having input into all aspects of the program. One youth described this as "the ability to make changes and design our own space" (Lindsay, Pollack, Pellegrino, & Cole, 2002, p. 13).

Clearly, students are more than wards whose custody is shared between school and afterschool programs. Their hearts and minds supply the energy, and much of the direction, to the educative process.

Conclusion

The emerging field of afterschool programming opens up exciting possibilities for educators. We believe not only that afterschool programs are capable of contributing greatly to the education of our children in appropriate and successful ways, but that such programs also find themselves in an ideal position to richly and fully engage the participation of children, youth, and families. Afterschool programs have the potential to allow students to define the goals of their own learning, and to help them meaningfully connect learning experiences to the social context of their families and communities. As we pointed out in the Introduction, afterschool programs also offer an ideal means of bridging gaps between parents and schools, schools and children, and schools and the wider community in order to overcome the dissociation of children's multiple worlds.

This book has grappled with some of the crucial challenges to afterschool learning and has offered recommendations for practices, policies, and further research. As we proceeded in our examination of building bridges between schools and afterschool programs and communities, extended learning through homework, and enriched learning through curricula, we have been constantly reminded of the complexity of the tasks at hand. Obviously, we have not exhausted our topics, nor have we been able to touch upon other topics crucial to afterschool learning, such as tutor training and supervision or the use of new technology in learning. We are currently developing an agenda for research and development around the central themes of this book and are further developing a strategy for technical assistance and quality improvement in the area of learning beyond school. Harvard's five-year commitment to this effort, in close collaboration with other organizations and institutions, will provide us with the time we will need to create tools, evaluate their efficacy, and support the training of teachers and staff to contribute to the further enhancement of afterschool, not only locally, but nationally and even internationally. By defining the goals of learning in afterschool, we may also refine our understanding of precisely what supports and scaffolding children need to achieve academically, and what extra mentoring and tutoring vulnerable children require so they will not be left behind.

Overall, our research and thinking lead us to recommend the following principles as a basic framework for guiding and enhancing learning in afterschool:

- Develop tools and methods that can be deployed nationally across a range of different afterschool environments.
- Make focused attempts, consonant with program goals, to support the goals of parents by aligning afterschool with the school day, while carefully maintaining the difference between school and afterschool time.
- Create programming continuities from the school and its curriculum and goals to the afterschool, and use afterschool to positively affect children's school-day performance.
- Seize upon all available opportunities to reinsert families and communities into children's experience of learning, simultaneously helping children acquire knowledge about their environment and their heritage as well as state-mandated subject matter.
- Support children's developmental and learning capacities by reducing their health and mental health risks.
- Invest in staff training, which means also to create careers in afterschool education, establish a fair compensation structure, and promote career paths for various types of education specialists.
- Invest in systematic research to build a system of learning that is firmly evidence based.

Beyond these basic principles, a range of important questions opens up before practitioners, policymakers, and researchers: What homework supports generate the best success? To what extent do projects enhance academic outcomes and motivation for learning? What level of structure for academic curricula is best for which age groups and types of children? How do we define and evaluate the learning that goes on in afterschool that standardized tests will never be able to measure? How do we integrate special needs children in afterschool learning? These are only a few of the many urgent questions we now confront as afterschool educators. We are still a long way from crystallizing the field through careful definitions and frameworks, evolved model programs and projects, and detailed longitudinal research, but this book represents a step into a more refined and integrated exchange of ideas and research.

In order to succeed, afterschool programs require an infusion of technical assistance, collaboration, and funding that will help to create infrastructures. At the moment, it is particularly important that afterschool programs build on their strengths, rather than dwelling upon deficiencies or problems. The topics we have chosen to focus upon in this book—building bridges, homework, and enriched learning through curricula—are so closely interrelated that an improvement in one area inevitably creates gains in other areas. For example, improving bridging between schools and afterschool programs helps to refine homework help and tutoring. Likewise, enriched learning through project-based curricula will enhance students' general attitude and academic performance during the school day. We stress the fact that not everything can be done at once, yet small steps will produce large results.

Although we hold great hopes for the burgeoning field of afterschool education, we would be remiss if we did not close with a note of caution. Those who work in the afterschool field know from experience that afterschool impacts children in ways both great and small. Afterschool programs that run the gamut from exclusively academic to exclusively recreational can succeed and fail for reasons that have only partially to do with their bridging, homework practices, and curricula. Rather, the success or failure of programs has everything to do with the extent to which they create buy-in from youth through engaging programming and, perhaps most importantly, through respectful, reciprocal relationships.

The second main caution for us all is to guard against getting carried away by our optimism for the field. While afterschool education does hold incredible promise, it is crucial that we acknowledge its inherent challenges. Until afterschool staff are professionalized and receive salaries commensurate with the important work they do, we will continue to face the challenge of a transient work force. This fundamental truth affects the effectiveness of professional development, regardless of its amount or extent. More than one interviewee spoke of the worries they had about the afterschool field underestimating the difficulty of academic remediation and overestimating the capacities of an underpaid, uncredentialed work force. Furthermore, most programs work in near isolation from one another, making it nearly impossible to share lessons learned and resources found. Thus, the very infrastructure of the afterschool field limits the amount of hope we should place upon its shoulders. It is our hope that this text and its advocacy for strengthening afterschool's infrastructure while maintaining its unique spirit may help to shape the goals set for the field, by those both within the field and outside it.

Given the rapidly accelerating pace of afterschool education as a serious area of study, we are in a great position to bring creativity, exploration, and informed practice to all aspects of afterschool learning. By answering the burning questions confronting us in our attempt to define the best possible use of out-of-school time, we will find that we have simultaneously enlarged the school reform debate. Afterschool programming has the potential to raise the achievement level of all participating children and youth, while creating the foundations for lifelong curiosity and experimentation with knowledge. We regard afterschool environments as flexible, intermediary spaces capable of supporting rich learning experiences and connecting the many worlds of children.

Appendix A

Context

U.S. Department of Education and the Mott Foundation

On the national level, a private-public partnership has proven to be enormously successful in helping shape the field of afterschool education and care. The U.S. Department of Education (DOE) and the Mott Foundation have partnered to create increased funding, infrastructure, and quality for afterschool programming. The DOE has received increased funding appropriations at a staggering pace. In 1998 Congress approved $40 million, and in 2002 this amount increased to $1 billion. Both the Mott Foundation and the DOE are making learning in afterschool settings an important priority. The Office of Educational Research and Improvement, under the auspices of the DOE, published a guide for *Bringing Education to After-school Programs* (1999) that illustrates the extent to which the DOE wishes to clarify and strengthen learning goals in the afterschool hours. In 2000, the Department of Justice and the DOE issued a paper, entitled *Working for Children and Families: Safe and Smart After-school Programs*, that delineates the importance of afterschool learning in children's academic and overall development. In January of 2002, the Mott Foundation and the DOE convened an expert group in Washington, DC, to begin to formulate a research and practice agenda for strengthening the learning goals of programs across the country.

Boston Afterschool for All Partnership

The work of the Boston Afterschool for All Partnership was a significant impetus for undertaking this book. The Partnership is notable as the largest public and private partnership in the city's history (Delawala, 2001), illustrating the importance of afterschool in the public and political agenda.

Afterschool for All represents a commitment by 15 organizations to disperse at least $23 million in new grants to significantly expand the quantity and quality of afterschool programming in Boston over the next five years. Though each partner is free to make grants according to its priorities, three overarching goals were identified for the initiative: 1) expansion of the number of children programs can serve by at least 5,000; 2) increased sustainability of programs by significantly increasing streams of public revenue to fund a system of afterschool and summer programs; and 3) improved academic achievement and positive development of children by supporting afterschool and summer providers in integrating high-yield learning activities into programs.

It is this last priority, currently being defined, that has provided an important motivation for our research and for this report. Chris Gabrieli, chairman of the Partnership, emphasizes the positive connection between afterschool programs and children's healthy development and educational achievement. He states that the Partnership hopes to raise public awareness of afterschool's impact, thereby generating further political attention and ensuring a sustainable funding stream. As afterschool is receiving increased public attention, program quality, specifically in regard to academic outcomes, has become increasingly important. The Boston Partnership was initiated by and works closely with Mayor Thomas M. Menino. His 2:00-to-6:00 After-School Initiative has as its mission "to support the expansion of high-quality after-school programming across the city, providing new learning and development opportunities for children." Harvard University's After School Initiative (see below) and PAER work closely with both organizations and their managing directors, Deborah McLaughlin and Kathleen Traphagen.

Cambridge's Agenda for Children

In Cambridge, Massachusetts, a strong organizing movement is also under way, which is called the Agenda for Children. The Agenda is an initiative of the Coordinating Council for Children, Youth, and Families (a Cambridge city board) dedicated to positively impacting issues of family well-being and child development through policy recommendations and program enhancement and expansion. After an extensive goal-setting and planning process during which a diverse cross-section of stakeholders was consulted, the Agenda for Children identified two central goals:

1) All children and their families in Cambridge will be able to read.
2) Children and youth will have access to safe, stimulating, nurturing, and healthful out-of-school time activities.

To achieve the second objective, the city has hired an out-of-school time co-ordinator, Susan Richards Scott, who works closely with Jackie Neel and Ellen Semonoff at the Department of Human Services, and the school su-perintendent has begun to establish program support networks, enhanced professional development and technical assistance, and accessible informa-tion systems for families. All of this activity is bringing Cambridge closer to achieving a vision of coordinated, high-quality service provision in out-of-school time. We have begun to work with Cambridge programs to strengthen their educational and mental health support. Our experiences with this work are also reflected in this book.

Harvard After-School Initiative (HASI)

As part of Harvard's efforts to develop new opportunities for university-community collaboration, the university has established the Harvard After School Initiative (HASI). HASI is affiliated with the Boston Afterschool for All Partnership and is administered by Kevin McCluskey and Jane Corlette of the Office of Government, Community, and Public Affairs under the leadership of vice president Alan Stone. It brings together three organiza-tions—the Program in Afterschool Education and Research, the Harvard Children's Initiative, and the Philips Brooks House Association—around grant-making, volunteerism, and technical assistance. HASI is particularly dedicated to building on the good work already under way in afterschool programs in the Allston-Brighton, Fenway, and Mission Hill sections of Boston. A first round of grant-making has recently ended, supported by consultants Andrew Bundy and Elaine Fersh.

Program in Afterschool Education and Research

The Harvard Graduate School of Education created the Program in After-school Education and Research (PAER), which is dedicated to making meaningful theoretical and practical contributions to the field of youth development and afterschool programs through community partnerships, curriculum and professional development, and research and evaluation initiatives. PAER's mission centers around three priorities: understanding and enhancing the learning opportunities for youth in afterschool programs; support and training around issues of youth mental health and well-being; and increasing the visibility of out-of-school time as a field of academic study and research. HASI and PAER represent new models for university-community collaborations that apply the academic and financial resources of the university to the improvement of community-based youth services. For more information, please see the PAER website (http://www.PAERweb. org). PAER, with its mission to strengthen the academic foundation of afterschool education and to focus on research, policy, and training to increase learning opportunities and mental health, has also begun its own journal entitled *New Directions in Youth Development: Theory, Practice and Research,* published by Jossey-Bass. The summer 2000 issue was dedicated to citywide initiatives in afterschool time and represents a companion piece to this book for the reader who wants to have an overview of the field.

Appendix B

Statistics about Boston and Cambridge Communities

The following demographic information provides a general overview of the communities that are referenced in this book. For further information, please see the Boston and Cambridge Redevelopment Authority websites at www.cityofboston.gov/BRA and www.ci.cambridge.ma.us/~CDD/data/, respectively. The following information is from these sources unless otherwise noted.

The city of Boston has a population of 589,141, 18.7 percent of whom live below the poverty line (U.S. Census Bureau, 2000). Youths between the ages of five and 14 make up 11.2 percent, or 66,274, of this population. As Table 1 shows, the homes of these youth represent a richness and diversity of races, ethnicities, and cultural origins. In fact, almost one-half of Boston's population is part of a "minority" group. Over one-quarter of Boston's population has immigrated from other countries, half of those in the last decade. And about one-third of Boston's population speaks a language other than English in the home.

According to 1990 Census figures, Harvard's three host communities are home to approximately 6,000 youths between ages five and 14, distributed as follows: Fenway, 626; Allston-Brighton, 3,552; Mission Hill, 1,797. Table 2 details race and ethnicity information for these neighborhoods in 1990. In the host communities, the percentages of households living at poverty level are: Fenway, 36.1 percent; Allston-Brighton, 20.1 percent; and Mission Hill, 41.0 percent.

Boston has approximately 234 afterschool programs serving elementary and middle school–aged youth (Boston School-Age Child Care Project, 2001). Of these, about 43 percent also serves youths more than 13 years old. Approximately 30 percent of the programs are based in schools, although

TABLE 1   *Sums and Percentages of Total Residents (adults and children) in Boston by Race, Culture, Origin, and First Language*

	Number	Percentage
Race (n = 589,141)		
White	320,944	54.5%
Black	149,202	25.3%
Native American	2,365	0.4%
Asian	44,284	7.5%
Pacific Islander	366	0.1%
Other	46,102	7.8%
Hispanic Origin (n = 589,141)	85,089	14.4%
Foreign Born (n = 589,141)	151,836	25.8%
Entered between 1990 and March 2000	73,670	12.5%
Language Spoken at Home (n = 557,376)		
English	371,185	66.6%
Other than English	186,191	33.4%
Spanish	75,711	13.6%

Source: U.S. Census Bureau (2000).

many of these are sponsored by community-based organizations. The Fenway, Allston-Brighton, and Mission Hill are extremely varied in terms of number of programs each has. Fenway has three, Mission Hill (depending on how the borders are drawn) has five, and Allston-Brighton has 24.

The City of Cambridge has a population of 101,355 people, of which 7,266 are youths between the ages of five and 14 (U.S. Census Bureau, 2000). Of this group, 48 percent qualify for free lunch in the public schools, and the racial breakdown is as follows: 40 percent White, 23 percent African American, 14 percent Hispanic, 11 percent Other Black, 11 percent Asian American, and 1 percent Native American (Office of Development and Assessment, 2001).

TABLE 2 *Sums and Percentages of All Residents (adults and children) in Harvard University's Boston Host Communities by Race and Ethnicity*

	Fenway	Mission Hill	Allston- Brighton	City of Boston
White	24,765	5,574	55,053	361,513
	75%	42.3%	78%	63%
Black	3,613	4,190	5,119	146,895
	11%	32%	7%	26%
Native American	88	82	236	1,965
	0.3%	0.6%	0.3%	0.3%
Asian/ Pacific Islander	3,128	1,096	7,694	38,457
	10%	8%	11%	7%
Hispanic Origin	2,419	3,337	6,091	59,892
	7%	25%	9%	10%
Other	1,269	2,222	2,281	38,457
	4%	17%	3%	7%
TOTALS	**32,893**	**13,164**	**70,383**	**574,283**

Source: Bundy (2001); based on 1990 U.S. Census data.

Susan Richards Scott from the Cambridge Agenda for Children esti- mates that there are approximately 72 afterschool programs in Cambridge serving children from kindergarten through grade seven. Of these, 49 are located in schools, while 23 are based in the community (S. Richards Scott, personal communication, February 20, 2002).

Appendix C

List of Interviews

TABLE 1 *Names and Affiliations of Interviewees*

Name	*Position*	*Organization*	*City, State*
Jenny Atkinson	Senior Director Education and the Arts	Boys & Girls Clubs of America	Atlanta, GA
Tina Blythe	Project Manager	Harvard Project Zero	Cambridge, MA
Juli Brownrigg	Kits Manager	Children's Museum	Boston, MA
Judy Caplan	Senior Program Associate	North Central Regional Educational Laboratory	Naperville, IL
An-Me Chung	Senior Programs Officer	Charles Stewart Mott Foundation	Flint, MI
Darlene Currie	After School Intermediary	Center for Collaborative Solutions	Sacramento, CA
Bobbi D'Allesandro	Superintendent	Cambridge Public Schools	Cambridge, MA
Alex Danesco	Associate Director	West End House Boys & Girls Club	Allston-Brighton, MA
Adriana de Kanter	Education Program Specialist	Office of Elementary and Secondary Education, U.S. Department of Education	Washington, DC

Sister Mary Duke	Principal	Our Lady of the Presentation School	Boston, MA
Matthew Farley	Interim Director	Harvard GEAR UP	Boston, MA
Andria Fletcher	After School Intermediary	Center for Collaborative Solutions	Sacramento, CA
Tim Garvin	Vice President & Executive Director	YMCA	Boston, MA
Varsha Ghosh	Director of Programs	Phillips Brooks House Association	Cambridge, MA
Marta Gredler	Program Manager	Parents United for Child Care	Boston, MA
Bob Healy	City Manager	City of Cambridge	Cambridge, MA
Erica Herman	Director	Gardner Extended Services School	Allston-Brighton, MA
Jill Herold	Executive Director	Cambridge Department of Human Services Programs	Cambridge, MA
Lenora Jennings	Director	Student Achievement & Accountability	Cambridge, MA
Ben Kirshner	Doctoral Candidate	Cooperative Research in Education, Stanford University	Stanford, CA
Kitty Kramer	School Age Childcare Manager	Cambridge Department of Human Services	Cambridge, MA
David Maher	City Councilor	City of Cambridge	Cambridge, MA
Dishon Mills	After School Programs Coordinator, Curriculum & Instruction	Boston Public Schools	Boston, MA

Stephanie Mines	Site Coordinator	Fenway Afterschool Care Program	Fenway, MA
Terri Mulks	Director of Child Care Programs	Oak Square YMCA	Allston-Brighton, MA
Pilar O'Cadiz	Executive Director	Collaborative After School Project, University of California	Irvine, CA
Pam Ogletree	Program Officer	BELL Foundation & Basics Tutorial at Jackson Mann	Allston-Brighton, MA
Sam Piha	Director	San Francisco Beacon School Initiative	San Francisco, CA
Kristen Pineo	Education Director	West End House Boys & Girls Club	Allston-Brighton, MA
Tim Porter	Natural Science Developer	Children's Museum	Boston, MA
Leonardo T. Radomile	Executive Director	Renaissance Learning Program	Lexington, KY
Kenneth Reeves	City Councilor	City of Cambridge	Cambridge, MA
Tom Regan	Director of Afterschool	Jackson Mann Community Center	Allston-Brighton, MA
Elizabeth Reisner	Principal	Policy Studies Associates	Washington, DC
Susan Richards Scott	Coordinator	Cambridge Agenda for Children	Cambridge, MA
Joel Rubin	Teacher Resource Center Director	New England Aquarium	Boston, MA
Steve Seidel	Director	Harvard Project Zero	Cambridge, MA
Eve Shapiro	Site Coordinator	Hamilton Afterschool at Jackson Mann Community Center	Allston-Brighton, MA

Christine Shonhart	Children's Librarian	Allston-Brighton Library	Allston-Brighton, MA
Sister Helen Sullivan	Education Director	Jackson Mann Community Center	Allston-Brighton, MA
Carlos Swaby	Program Director	Rainbow Reading and Math, Madison Park	Mission Hill, MA
Maria Tempesta-Rios	Director	Fanueil Afterschool Program	Allston-Brighton, MA
Alice Turkel	Member	Cambridge School Committee & Kids' Council	Cambridge, MA
Leigh Van Dyken	RALLY Coordinator	Taft Middle School RALLY Program	Allston-Brighton, MA
Michael Ware	Director	Mission Hill Community Centers, Tobin School Age Child Care	Mission Hill, MA
Laura Warner	RALLY Coordinator	Taft Middle School RALLY Program	Allston-Brighton, MA
Robert Weinstein	Deputy Director of Training & Technical Assistance	The After-School Corporation	New York, NY
Richard Weissbourd	Lecturer on Education/ Cofounder	Harvard Graduate School of Education/ ReadBoston	Cambridge, MA
Laura Wolhafe	Curriculum Development Specialist	Foundations, Inc.	Mount Laurel, NJ
Marinelle Yoders	Program Officer	Boston 2:00-to-6:00 Initiative	Boston, MA

Additional Discussions That Have Influenced the Content of This Book

Anthony Appiah, Harvard University, Cambridge, MA

Milli Pierce, Principals' Center, Harvard Graduate School of Education, Cambridge, MA

Imma deStephanis, Harvard Children's Initiative, Cambridge, MA

Jacquelynne S. Eccles, University of Michigan at Ann Arbor

Elaine Fersh and Andrew Bundy, Community Matters, Watertown, MA, and
    Providence, RI

Jose Figueriedo, Charles G. Harrington School, Cambridge, MA

Kurt Fischer, Harvard Graduate School of Education, Cambridge, MA

Lucy Friedman, The After-School Corporation, New York, NY

Christopher Gabrieli, Massachusetts 2020, chair, Boston Afterschool for All Partnership,
    Boston, MA

Greater Boston Interfaith Organization, Education Committee, Boston, MA

Ron and Cyndie Haan, Haan Foundation for Children, San Francisco, CA

Dr. Hanscom, Grover Cleveland Middle School, Dorchester, MA

Carrie Hickie, Taft Middle School, Allston-Brighton, MA

Robert Halpern, Erikson Institute for Graduate Study in Child Development, Chicago, IL

Robert Kargman, Boston Land Company, Boston, MA

Judith Kidd, Philips Brooks House Association, Harvard University, Cambridge, MA

Tim Knowles, Boston Public Schools, Boston, MA

Kevin McCluskey, Harvard University Office of Government, Community, and Public
    Affairs, Cambridge, MA

Deborah McLaughlin, Boston Afterschool for all Partnership, Boston, MA

Milbrey McLaughlin, Stanford University, Stanford, CA

Joel Monell, Harvard Graduate School of Education, Cambridge, MA

Pedro Noguera, Harvard Graduate School of Education, Cambridge, MA

Judith Palfrey, Harvard Children's Initiative, Cambridge, MA

Sophia Piexoto, Harrington Extended Day Program, Cambridge, MA

Ellen Semenoff, Cambridge Department of Human Service Programs, Cambridge, MA

Eric Schwarz and Ned Rimer, Citizen Schools, Boston, MA

David Shapps, Developmental Studies Center, Oakland, CA

Herb Sturz, Open Society Institute, New York, NY

Kathleen Traphagen, Boston 2:00-to-6:00 Initiative, Boston, MA

Heather Weiss, Harvard Family Research Project, Cambridge, MA

Daniel Wilson, Project Zero, Harvard University, Cambridge, MA

Julius Wilson, John F. Kennedy School of Government, Harvard University,
    Cambridge, MA

References

Aikenhead, G. H. (1996). Science education: Border crossing into the subculture of science. *Studies in Science Education, 27*, 1–52.

Amundson, K. J. (1995). *Brush up your study skills: Tips for students and parents.* Arlington, VA: American Association of School Administrators.

Au, K. H. (1980). Participant structures in a reading lesson with Hawaiian children: Analysis of a culturally appropriate instructional event. *Anthropology and Education Quarterly, 11*, 91–115.

Au, K. H., & Mason, J. (1981). Social organization factors in learning to read: The balance of rights hypothesis. *Reading Research Quarterly, 17*, 115–152.

Bain & Company. (1998). *The Bain report.* Boston: Boston 2:00-to-6:00 Initiative.

Ball, A., & Heath, S. B. (1993). Dances of identity: Finding an ethnic self in the arts. In S. B. Heath & M. W. McLaughlin (Eds.), *Identity and inner-city youth: Beyond ethnicity and gender* (pp. 69–93). New York: Teachers College Press.

Blythe, T., Boyd, J., Wilson, D., & Noam, G. (2002). *Fun learning matters! A guide to doing projects in afterschool programs.* Unpublished manuscript, Project Zero and PAER, Harvard University, Cambridge, MA.

Boston School-Age Child Care Project. (2001). *2001 guide to Boston's before and after school programs: Serving elementary and middle school students and their families.* Boston: Parents United for Child Care.

Bundy, A. L. (2001). *Building on strengths: Out-of-school time opportunities and challenges for children and youth in three Boston neighborhoods. Scanning community assets, resources and concerns in Allston-Brighton, Mission Hill, and the Fenway.* Watertown, MA: Bundy & Associates.

Calabrese, R. L. (1990). The public school: A source of alienation for minority parents. *Journal of Negro Education, 59*, 148–154.

Children's Museum & Boston 2:00-to-6:00 Initiative. (2000). *The Expanding Youth Horizons Initiative: Supporting learning in Boston after-school programs.* Boston: Barr Foundation.

Clark, R. M. (1992). Why disadvantaged students succeed. *Connections,* (Summer), 10–13.

Clement, J., Lauer, R. H., & Wolhafe, L. (2000). *Foundations travels.* Mount Laurel, NJ: Foundations.

Cooper, H. M. (2001a). *The battle over homework: Common ground for administrators, teachers, and parents.* Thousand Oaks, CA: Corwin Press.

Cooper, H. M. (2001b). Homework for all—in moderation. *Educational Leadership, 58*(7), 34–38.

Cooperative Artists Institute. (2000). *Tribal Rhythms.* Jamaica Plain, MA: Author.

Davidson, A. L. (1999). Negotiating social differences: Youths' assessments of educators' strategies. *Urban Education, 34,* 338–369.

Davis, J., & Farbman, D. (2002). Schools alone are not enough: After-school programs and education reform in Boston. In G. G. Noam & B. M. Miller (Eds.), *Youth development and after-school time: A tale of many cities. New Directions for Youth Development* (pp. 65–88). San Francisco: Jossey Bass.

De Kanter, A., Huff, M., & Chung, A. M. (2002, May 17–18). *Supplementation vs. supplantation: What is the core of schooling and what is supplemental?* Paper presented at the conference entitled After-School Programs and Supplementary Education, New York.

Delawala, I. (2001, March 14). Harvard to back afterschool initiative today. *Harvard Crimson,* p. 1.

Delgado-Gaitan, C. (1987). Traditions and transitions in the learning process of Mexican children: An ethnographic view. In G. Spindler & L. Spindler (Eds.), *Interpretive ethnography of education: At home and abroad* (pp. 333–359). Hillsdale, NJ: Lawrence Erlbaum.

Delpit, L. D. (1995). *Other people's children: Cultural conflict in the classroom.* New York: New Press.

Developmental Studies Center. (2000). *KidzLit.* Oakland, CA: Author.

Dewey, J. (1916). *Democracy and education: An introduction to the philosophy of education.* New York: Macmillan.

Eccles, J. (1999). The development of children ages 6 to 14. *Future of Children, 9*(2), 30–44.

Erickson, F. D. (1993). Transformation and school success: The politics and culture of educational achievement. In E. Jacob & C. Jacob (Eds.), *Minority education: Anthropological perspectives* (pp. 27–52). Norwood, NJ: Ablex.

Erickson, F. D., & Mohatt, G. (1982). Cultural organization in two classrooms of Indian students. In G. D. Spindler (Ed.), *Doing the ethnography of schooling: Educational anthropology in action* (pp. 132–175). New York: Holt, Rinehart & Winston.

Gardner, H. (1991). *The unschooled mind: How children think and how schools should teach.* New York: Basic Books.

Gardner, H. (1999). *Intelligence reframed: Multiple intelligences for the 21ˢᵗ century.* New York: Basic Books.

Glazer, N. T., & Williams, S. (2001). Averting the homework crisis. *Educational Leadership, 58*(7), 43–45.

Gordon, E. W. (1979). New perspectives on old issues. In D. A. Wilkerson (Ed.), *Educating all our children: An imperative for democracy* (pp. 52–75). Westport, CT: Mediax.

Grant, C. A., & Sleeter, C. E. (1996). *After the school bell rings.* Washington, DC: Falmer Press.

Halpern, R. (1999). After-school programs for low-income children: Promises and challenges. *Future of Children, 9*(2), 81–95.

Heath, S. B. (1982). Questioning at school and at home: A comparative study. In G. D. Spindler (Ed.), *Doing the ethnography of schooling: Educational anthropology in action* (pp. 102–131). New York: Holt, Rinehart & Winston.

Heath, S. B. (1992). The project of learning from the inner-city youth perspective. In F. A. Villarruel & R. M. Lerner (Eds.), *Promoting community-based programs for socialization and learning* (pp. 25–34). San Francisco: Jossey-Bass.

Hong, E., & Milgram, R. M. (2000). *Homework: Motivation and learning preference.* Westport, CT: Bergin & Garvey.

John, V. P. (1972). Styles of learning—styles of teaching: Reflections on the education of Navajo children. In C. B. Cazden, V. P. John, & D. Hymes (Eds.), *Functions of language in the classroom* (pp. 331–343). New York: Teachers College Press.

John, V. P., & Leacock, E. (1979). Transforming the structure of failure. In D. A. Wilkerson (Ed.), *Educating all our children: An imperative for democracy* (pp. 76–91). Westport, CT: Mediax.

Juel, C. (1996). What makes literacy tutoring effective? *Reading Research Quarterly, 31,* 268–289.

Katz, L. G., & Chard, S. C. (2000). *Engaging children's minds: The project approach* (2nd ed.). Stamford, CT: Ablex.

Kralovec, E., & Buell, J. (2000). *The end of homework: How homework disrupts families, overburdens children, and limits learning.* Boston: Beacon Press.

Larson, R. W. (2000). Toward a psychology of positive youth development. *American Psychologist, 55*(1), 170–183.

Lindsay, J., Pollack, S., Pellegrino, M., & Cole, K. (2002). *After-school programs in Boston: What young people think and want.* Boston: Center for Teen Empowerment.

Marzano, R. J. (2001). *Classroom instruction that works: Research-based strategies for increasing student achievement.* Alexandria, VA: Association for Supervision and Curriculum Development.

Massachusetts 2020. (2002). *No time to lose: Children and their afterschool hours.* Boston: Keeping Kids on Track Campaign. Retrieved January 24, 2002, from http://www.kkot.org/presentation/Survey%20Results%20(Final%20Version) _files/frame.htm

McLaughlin, M., Irby, M., & Langman, J. (1994). *Urban sanctuaries: Neighborhood organizations in the lives of inner-city youth.* San Francisco: Jossey Bass.

McLaughlin, M. W. (1993). Embedded identities: Enabling balance in urban contexts. In S. B. Heath & M. W. McLaughlin (Eds.), *Identity and inner-city youth: Beyond gender and ethnicity* (pp. 36–68). New York: Teachers College Press.

Moll, L. C., & Diaz, S. (1993). Change as a goal of educational research. In E. Jacob & C. Jacob (Eds.), *Minority education: Anthropological perspectives* (pp. 67–82). Norwood, NJ: Ablex.

National Parent Teacher Association & National Education Association. (2000). *Helping your student get the most out of homework.* Retrieved July 18, 2001, from http://www.pta.org/programs/edulibr/homework.htm

Noam, G. (2001, May). *Afterschool time: Toward a theory of collaboration.* Paper presented at the Urban Seminar Series on Children's Mental Health and Safety: Out of School Time, Cambridge, MA.

Noam, G., & Miller, B.

Noam, G., Winner, K., Rhein, A., & Molad, B. (1996). The Harvard RALLY program and the prevention practitioner: Comprehensive, school-based intervention to support resiliency in at-risk adolescents. *Journal of Child and Youth Care Work, 11,* 32–47.

Noam, G. G., Pucci, K., & Foster, E. (1999). Development, resilience, and school success in youth: The prevention practitioner and the Harvard RALLY program. In D. Cicchetti & S. Toth (Eds.), *Developmental approaches to prevention and intervention* (pp. 57–109). Rochester, NY: University of Rochester Press.

O'Connor, S., & McGuire, K. (1998). *Homework assistance & out-of-school time: Filling the need, finding a balance. The MOST Initiative.* Wellesley, MA: National Institute on Out-of-School Time.

Office of Development and Assessment. (2001). *Elementary (K–8) report for school year 2000–2001.* Cambridge, MA: Cambridge Public Schools.

Office of Educational Research and Improvement & U.S. Department of Education. (1999). *Bringing education to after-school programs.* Washington, DC: U.S. Government Printing Office.

Ogbu, J. U. (1987). Variability in minority responses to schooling: Nonimmigrants vs. immigrants. In G. Spindler & L. Spindler (Eds.), *Interpretive ethnography of education: At home and abroad* (pp. 255–278). Hillsdale, NJ: Lawrence Erlbaum.

Paulu, N. (1995). *Helping your child with homework: For parents of elementary and junior high school-aged children.* Washington, DC: U.S. Department of Education.

PCS Edventures.COM. (2002). *The academy of engineering labs.* Boise, ID: PCS Education Systems.

Phelan, P., Davidson, A. L., & Yu, H. C. (1998). *Adolescents' worlds: Negotiating family, peers, and school.* New York: Teachers College Press.

Posner, J. K., & Vandell, D. L. (1994). Low-income children's after-school care: Are there beneficial effects of after-school programs? *Child Development, 65,* 440–456.

Posner, J. K., & Vandell, D. L. (1999). After-school activities and the development of low-income urban children: A longitudinal study. *Developmental Psychology, 35,* 868–879.

Schinke, S., Cole, K., & Poulin, S. (2000). Enhancing the educational achievement of at-risk youth. *Prevention Science, 1,* 51–60.

Scribner, S., & Cole, M. (1973). Cognitive consequences of formal and informal education. *Science, 182,* 553–559.

Snow, C. E., Barnes, W., Chandler, J., Hemphill, L., & Goodman, I. (1991). *Unfulfilled expectations: Home and school influences on literacy.* Cambridge, MA: Harvard University Press.

Snow, C. E., Burns, M. S., & Griffin, P. (Eds.). (1998). *Preventing reading difficulties in young children.* Washington, DC: National Academy Press.

Spindler, G. D. (1997). Why have minority groups in North America been disadvantaged by their schools? In G. D. Spindler (Ed.), *Education and cultural process: Anthropological approaches* (pp. 96–109). Prospect Heights, IL: Waveland.

Steppingstone Foundation. (n.d.). *About Steppingstone.* Retrieved July 2, 2002, from http://www.tsf.org/about/abt.html

U.S. Census Bureau. (2000). *U.S. Census 2000.* Retrieved February 14, 2002, from http://www.census.gov/main/www/cen2000.html

U.S. Department of Justice & U.S. Department of Education. (2000). *Working for children and families: Safe and smart after-school programs.* Washington, DC: U.S. Government Printing Office.

WhaleNet. (2001). *Lucy, the inflatable whale.* Retrieved February 8, 2002, from http://whale.wheelock.edu/whalenet-stuff/LucyPage.html

Work Family Directions (WFD). (2000). *Welcome to the Activities Club Homework and Edutainment Club!* Boston: Author.

Youth Development Institute. (1997). *Beacons and afterschool education: Making literacy links.* New York: Fund for the City of New York.

Commentaries

Globalization and the Democratic Space: Why What Happens After School Matters

Marcelo M. Suárez-Orozco

Harvard University

In this commentary, I examine globalization and reflect on its implications for learning in afterschool settings. The basic question I pose is, how do we raise children to grow up and thrive in a world where global forces will increasingly come to the fore in structuring and shaping their opportunities, their identities, and the kinds of lives they will lead? By global forces, I mean the unprecedented changes in the economy, in society, and in our culture that are transforming the social environments in which children are growing up. A further theme in this reflection is how we think about the role of learning beyond schools and the role of afterschool settings as potential democratizing spaces in preparing children to develop the technical skills, social competencies, and cultural sensibilities that will be demanded of them by new global dynamics.

First, a word about globalization. Globalization can be conceptualized as processes of change structured by three fundamental, powerful, and, in some ways, new currents. The first of these is the deterritorialization of economic formations, with new powerful market forces bypassing nation-state boundaries. Under the regime of global capitalism, the production and distribution of goods and services, financial markets, and foreign direct investment are increasingly globalized.[1] As Moisés Naím has argued, September

---

1. According to the World Bank, a "growing share of what countries produce is sold to other foreigners as exports. Among rich or developed countries the share of international trade in total output (exports plus imports of goods relative to GDP) rose from 27 to 39 percent between 1987 and 1997. For the developing countries it rose from 10 to 17 percent" (World Bank, 2001, p. 1). Likewise, foreign direct investment, that is, firms making investments in other

11 has done little to subvert the momentum toward increased economic globalization, at least as indexed by international trade: "World trade is projected to grow by nearly 8 per cent in the second half of this year [2002] and by 10 per cent in the first six months of next year" (Naím, 2002, p. 10). These global economic processes suggest that the fortunes of children growing up today—whether they are in Boston, San Jose, or New Delhi— will be tied to economic formations that are increasingly postnational (Suárez-Orozco & Gardner, 2002).

Second, globalization is structured by the emergence of new information and communication technologies that allow people to communicate, work, and come together in ways that we have never seen before. In the age of the Internet, even highly authoritarian states find it a challenge to limit access to outside information, opinions, trends, and sensibilities. These new technologies also place a premium on knowledge-intensive work. Such technologies are going to be central to any understanding of child socialization in the new millennium—and of how to best prepare children for the new world.

The third new dynamic behind globalization is large-scale immigration. We are now in the middle of the largest wave of immigration in history. What is most striking is how fast the current wave of immigration gained its worldwide momentum. The number of immigrants has doubled from 1965 to 2000. Today, there are over 150 million international immigrants and refugees, plus an estimated 20 to 25 million people displaced within their nations of birth (Nyberg-Sørensen, Van Hear, & Engberg-Pedersen, 2002).

Immigration is not a Boston issue, a New York issue, or a Los Angeles issue. Immigration is a global force that is transforming the world. Frankfurt's population today is one-quarter immigrant, and the overall rate of immigration in Germany is now comparable to that of the United States. Rotterdam, the world's largest port, located in the heart of Europe, is now nearly 45 percent immigrant. The United States is in the middle of the largest wave of immigration in the country's history: in just two generations, it

countries, overall "more than tripled between 1988 and 1998 from US$ 192 billion to US$ 610 billion"(p. 1). From the time the reader woke up this morning to the time she goes to bed tonight, over a trillion dollars will have crossed national boundaries (Friedman, 2000).

will be the only postindustrial democracy in the world where roughly half of the population is a member of a so-called ethnic minority. The most astonishing data come from the growth of the Latino population: a 58 percent increase in just one decade. According to U.S. Census estimates, the United States will have about 100 million Latinos in two generations and will then have the second largest Latino-origin population in the world, after Mexico (Suárez-Orozco & Páez, 2002).

Why do we need to think about immigration and globalization in the context of afterschool programs? Immigrant children are now the fastest-growing sector of the U.S. child population. Roughly one in five children in the United States today is the child of an immigrant, and that figure is projected to be one in three by the year 2040 (Suárez-Orozco & Suárez-Orozco, 2001). How are these new dynamics shaping the lives and needs of our newly arrived immigrant children in and out of schools? What is the role of learning beyond school settings for this growing sector of our child population?

Afterschool sites have the potential to become effective democratizing spaces, redressing some of the inequities immigrant children of color face in many of our large inner-city school districts. This is an important challenge because, given the demographic processes at work, the education of new immigrants will be fundamental for the kind of cultural democracy we are going to become. Schools and afterschool programs will be strongly implicated in the long-term trajectories of these children.

Some immigrant children are thriving in schools. These children are more likely than ever before in the history of the United States to end up at Harvard College. More than half of all foreign-born East Asians in the United States have advanced degrees. The children of these highly educated and skilled immigrants are bypassing the traditional transgenerational modes of mobility, moving into middle-class status within a generation. But many children of immigrants and refugees, especially from the Caribbean, Latin America, and Southeast Asia, are struggling against the odds. Many are likely to end up under the supervision of the criminal justice system (Vigil, 2002). Approximately half of all children in the California Youth Authority today come from Latino homes. We have never seen this kind of intensified bifurcation in the trajectories of immigrant children. For many new arrivals it is "Yale or jail," as one of the informants in our longitudinal study put it.

Indeed, children of immigrants in record numbers are settling into social contexts where schools have not been successful at imparting the skills, competencies, and sensibilities needed in today's global economy. Many children of immigrants are encountering serious problems in our schools. About half of all Latino youth in the Texas schools (again, a large majority of these children are of immigrant origin) will not graduate from high school; nationwide, 30 percent of Latino children drop out school (Flores et al., 2002). This is at a time when the global economy is unforgiving of those who do not have the skills to compete in the knowledge-intensive sector of the economy. In the year 2000 the median hourly wage in the Boston area for a male Latino high school dropout was $10.00 ($8.00 for females) and the median hourly wage for a male Latino college graduate was $21.06 ($17.50 for females). Education pays more than ever.

In the Longitudinal Immigrant Student Adaptation Project, which is the largest research undertaking of its kind, we have found that immigrant parents from Asia, the Caribbean, and Latin America value education greatly (Suárez-Orozco & Suárez-Orozco, 2001). We have also found a great deal of resiliency in immigrant families. Immigrant families typically value hard work, privilege familism, and a share a general optimism about the future. Yet our data also suggest that many immigrant parents are unable to guide their children through the kinds of cultural models and social practices that seem critical to succeed in the new setting. This is again a very important domain to understand because family-level factors are directly related to the long-term trajectories of children. Preliminary findings from our research suggest that many immigrant parents cannot help their kids the way middle-class white, nonimmigrant parents typically do. In some cases it is as simple as not being able to help with homework. In other cases, it is not being able to deploy the cultural models or enact the social practices known to enhance a child's opportunities in school. Cultural models of school also vary greatly among groups. The American cultural model of the "parent as advocate" is foreign to many immigrant parents who may privilege a "teacher-knows-best" approach. Some immigrant parents value education and schooling but lack the complex cultural savoir faire and socioeconomic resources that are important in relating to schools.

Afterschool programs cannot solve all of the problems facing children of immigrants, but they can work to impart the skills and culturally coded forms of symbolic capital that immigrant children may not be able to generate at home. Tutoring reading, writing, mathematics, statistics, and test-taking is a domain in which afterschool programs can play a critical role. But mentors in afterschool settings can also play an important role in generating and transmitting forms of cultural capital that will be required if immigrant children are to become successful contributors to the kind of cultural democracy we are destined to become. The scaffolding provided by this book demonstrates the learning potential of afterschool programs and the millions of children that are being served through them.

In short, afterschool programs face the challenge to emerge as democratizing spaces servicing our littlest new Americans. Afterschool learning can help impart to immigrants and children of color the kinds of skills, including higher order cognitive skills, interpersonal sensibilities, and cultural competencies, that will be required for success in the new global world. Because of globalization, children growing today are more likely than any previous generation in human history to live, to learn, and eventually to work with others who are from backgrounds very different from their own. That is globalization's challenge to our school and afterschool programs.

References

Flores, G., Fuentes-Afflick, E., Barbot, O., Carter-Pokras, O., Claudio, L., Lara, M., McLaurin, J. A., Pachter, L., Gomez, F. G., Mendoza, F., Valdez, R. B., Villaruel, A. M., Zambrana, R. E., Greenberg, R., & Weitzman, M. (2002). The health of Latino children: Urgent priorities, unanswered questions, and a research agenda. *Journal of the American Medical Association, 288,* 82–90.

Friedman, T. (2000). *The Lexus and the olive tree: Understanding globalization.* New York: Anchor Books.

Naím, M. (2002, August 4). A complex and enduring globalisation. *Financial Times,* p. 10.

Nyberg-Sørensen, N., Van Hear, N., & Engberg-Pedersen, P. (2002). *The migration-development nexus: Evidence and policy options* (IOM Migration Research Series, No. 8). Retrieved August 12, 2002, from http://www.iom.int/documents/publication/en/mrs_8_2002.pdf

Suárez-Orozco, C., & Suárez-Orozco, M. (2001). *Children of immigration.* Cambridge, MA: Harvard University Press.

Suárez-Orozco, M., & Gardner, H. (2002, April). *Globalization and education.* Paper presented to the Seminar on Globalization and Education, Tarrytown, New York.

Suárez-Orozco, M., & Páez, M. (Eds.). (2002). *Latinos: Remaking America.* Berkeley: University of California Press.

Vigil, D. (2002). *Rainbow of gangs: Street culture in the Mega City.* Austin: University of Texas Press.

World Bank. (2001, April). *Assessing globalization.* Washington, DC: Author. Retrieved August 9, 2002, from http://www1.worldbank.org/economicpolicy/globalization/key_readings.html

Afterschool Education:
A Global Perspective

Reed Larson

University of Illinois at Urbana-Champaign

Globalization is spreading economic competition to every corner of the world, which affects both parents and young people. Labor markets are becoming international. As a result, parents' lives are speeding up—overheating, some might say. As they try to earn more or just keep up, they are transferring more and more of their parenting responsibilities to outside institutions: monitoring, chauffeuring, feeding, and now the supervising of their children's homework.

Young people are subject to the same competition. They are required to learn more and more in order to get into a good university and to compete for the knowledge-intensive jobs in the new economy. Competition for admission to the Ivy League has now become globalized, as has competition for the plum jobs in the Silicon Valleys of the world—or for any adequate, middle-class job. Globalization means that even learning-impaired students need to get more education because they are now competing with young people all over the world for the limited set of semi-skilled jobs, and the wages for those jobs are going down.

In Korea and India, where I have done research, this vortex of competition means that adolescents are spending increasing hours every day on schoolwork. In these nations, young people compete for a limited number of university slots, with selections based partly on school grades and partly on how students do on national college entrance examinations. To improve their exam performances, many go after school to a "cram school" or to a tutor, often until 8:00 or 9:00 at night. Our data show that the amount of time middle-class youths in these nations spend on schoolwork approaches 40 percent of waking hours (Lee & Larson, 2000; Verma, Sharma, & Larson, in press).

Young people, by and large, don't enjoy this time. They are not learning with excitement. In our studies with U.S. adolescents, we have found that students report being bored about 32 percent of the time (measured across random time samples).[1] During homework this approaches 40 percent of the time (Larson & Richards, 1991). Our research team has debated exactly what this means. Among the Inuit, the definition of fear is what you feel when you're standing in front of a polar bear. I think that sometimes for kids the definition of boredom is how you feel when you're doing schoolwork. I think it is also partly a posture of resistance, because schoolwork is something adults are making kids do. But it is also a real psychological state, one that affects how well children do that work and absorb the material.

This boredom with schoolwork is not unique to the United States. Across our data from the United States, India, and Korea, we have found a common profile during schoolwork, especially homework, that indicates that these activities are less than optimal experiences for young people. Students report having a higher challenge and higher concentration during homework compared to other activities in their lives, but they also report low motivation, difficulty in concentrating, and less than favorable emotional states. They report that they wish they were doing something else. Given the large amounts of time that young people in India and particularly Korea spend on homework, this starts to have a major influence on their emotional lives. We have found that Korean adolescents on average have markedly higher rates of clinical depression than American teens, and that those youths who spent the most time doing homework reported the most depressive symptoms (Lee & Larson, 2000)—presumably because they are getting the highest dosage of this experience.

The United States should not emulate this pattern, known in Korea as "the examination hell." But few parents in Korea, India, and other countries where testing is extremely important are willing to jeopardize their

1. These data are based on "beeper studies" with adolescents. At random times across waking hours, participants are signaled and asked to stop what they are doing to fill out a short report form. They report on whom they are with, what they are doing, what they are feeling, and how engaged they are at that moment. The goal of this research is to get snapshots of moments in teens' lives from their point of view.

children's future. There are commentaries in the press in India and Korea about how terrible this situation is, but no one seems willing to back out of it. I fear that politicians in the United States, with their promotion of high-stakes testing, are in danger of pushing our young people into the same sort of competitive vortex.

Members of our research group and others have concluded that the set of skills students are learning and being tested on in most schools today are only one of many important skill sets. In a sense, students are doing the *wrong* homework for life in the present and future. Other important skills that are crucial include the ability to think independently, to create structure in unstructured situations (which is what many of us do every day), to take initiative (i.e., to organize one's energies over time toward achieving a goal), to work in teams, and to cross boundaries—to function effectively across differences in ethnicity, profession, gender, and other factors (Larson, Brown, & Mortimer, 2002; Parker, Ninomiya, & Cogan, 1999).

Suárez-Orozco aptly termed this last skill set "transcultural forms of empathy." These are critical in the contemporary world because increasing numbers of people are working with colleagues from different cultural groups, living in multicultural neighborhoods, and even marrying or partnering with people who are from different cultures than their own. Of course, on a higher plane, cross-group conflict is a severe threat to existence in many parts of the world. From my point of view, the most important cultural curriculum across the world involves learning to bridge differences among people from various cultural worlds, religions, language communities, sexual identities, and occupational groups.

These very important skill sets are exactly those that are learned less by doing homework and more in goal-oriented, youth-centered afterschool programs (Larson, 2000; National Research Council, 2001). Japan, in fact, is trying to cut back on school pressures, adding more clubs and sports (Nishino & Larson, in press). Meanwhile, politicians in the United States are pushing us in the wrong direction, toward the wrong kinds of homework for the twenty-first century.

When we look at the subjective states that adolescents report during afterschool programs, we find the convergence of both concentration and motivation (Larson, 2000). During these activities, adolescents report feeling that they are challenged and concentrating hard. They are very motivated to be doing what they are doing; they are certainly not bored. Noam, Biancarosa, and Dechausay offer frameworks for shaping our understanding of how meaningful learning takes place in afterschool settings.

Effective afterschool programs provide both an important agenda of learning and the psychological conditions for that learning to occur. I am not antihomework. I know how crucial it is that students spend an adequate amount of time doing their lessons, and that we may no longer be able to depend on busy parents to ensure that this happens. But we need to make sure that schoolwork does not crowd out the important opportunities that afterschool programs provide—opportunities for young people to learn skills that are likely to be equally valuable, if not more valuable, in the years to come.

References

Larson, R. (2000). Towards a psychology of positive youth development. *American Psychologist, 55*, 170–183.

Larson, R., Brown, B. B., & Mortimer, J. (Eds.). (2002). Adolescents' preparation for the future: Perils and promise [Special Issue]. *Journal of Research on Adolescence, 12*, 1–166.

Larson, R., & Richards, M. (1991). Boredom in the middle school years: Blaming schools versus blaming students. *American Journal of Education, 91*, 418–443.

Lee, M., & Larson, R. (2000). The Korean "examination hell": Long hours of studying, distress, and depression. *Journal of Youth and Adolescence, 29*, 249–272.

National Research Council. (2001). *Community programs to promote youth development.* Washington, DC: National Academy Press.

Nishino, H. J., & Larson, R. (in press). Japanese adolescents' free time: Juku, Bukatsu, and government efforts to create more meaningful leisure. In S. Verma & R. Larson (Eds.), *International perspectives on the use of free time by adolescents.* San Francisco: Jossey-Bass.

Parker, W. C., Ninomiya, A., & Cogan, J. (1999). Educating world citizens: Toward multinational curriculum development. *American Educational Research Journal, 36*, 117–146.

Verma, S., Sharma, D., & Larson, R. (in press). School stress in India: Effects on time and daily emotions. *International Journal of Behavioral Development.*

Comments on Afterschool Programs: Bridging the School Day

Adriana de Kanter

U.S. Department of Education

The years 1996, 1997, and 1998 spawned an incredible confluence of like-mindedness about how to extend learning time, help working families, and keep children safe. There was a catalytic reaction from policymakers at the local, state, and federal levels that families needed options for their children in the afterschool time. Some of the major players in this new activity included The After-School Corporation (TASC) in New York City, Los Angeles' Better Education for Tomorrow Program (LA's BEST), Sacramento Start, San Diego's 6 to 6 Extended School Day Program, and Boston's 2:00-to-6:00 Afterschool Initiative. At the federal level, the 21st Century Community Learning Centers program was crafted into an afterschool program, growing from an initial appropriation of less than $1 million to a program now funded at $1 billion.

The U.S. Department of Education (DOE) has written about afterschool programs as a means of extending learning time, usually within the context of Title I remediation. The department's evaluation office has commissioned several studies and idea books on extended learning over the past 15 years, including the first national study of before- and afterschool time (Seppanen et al., 1993). It also produced a volume called *The Other 91 Percent* (Policy Studies Associates, 1993) as part of the national assessment of Chapter I in 1993 to lay out options for expanding learning and learning time.

The following year, the DOE released the congressionally mandated study *Prisoners of Time* (National Education Commission on Time and Learning, 1994). *Prisoners of Time* included several examples of what is described in *Afterschool Education: Approaches to an Emerging Field* as integrated afterschool programs. All programs in *Prisoners of Time* were school based and illustrated the point that school and afterschool could be not only successfully linked but also made seamless. However, in reviewing the afterschool literature of the last ten to 15 years, a focus on education and linking with the school day were always missing from what were considered the common elements of effective programs. So when the department released the document *Keeping Schools Open as Community Learning Centers* in 1997, it began to bring these concepts to the forefront of discussions in the emerging field (de Kanter, Fiester, Lauland, & Romney, 1997), and they were very controversial.

Still, the department was unwavering as it released a series of books called *Safe and Smart* (U.S. Department of Justice & U.S. Department of Education, 1998, 2000) that looked at the effectiveness of afterschool programs, and the common elements of effective programs, based on indicators of academic achievement, safety, and youth development. *Bringing Education to the After School Hours* (U.S. Department of Education, 1999) was then written, based on the concept that afterschool programs could link the regular school day content with the afterschool hours.

It was clear to the department that parents, kids, educators, and the public wanted children and youth to be involved in active learning in the afterschool time. And, as the 21st Century Community Learning Centers program developed, the department tried to provide guidance on how to deliver the smart side of *Safe and Smart* in its grantee training. But in reality, a discussion of the content and how to deliver it in quality afterschool programming was largely missing from this training, and from the burgeoning afterschool discussion.

Milbrey McLaughlin (2000) provided some insight into how to deliver content in *Community Counts* when she wrote about an embedded curriculum in the activities of youth-serving organizations. An-Me Chung of the Mott Foundation and I have also written about educational programming in the context of how to evaluate afterschool programs and the need to measure child learning outcomes (Chung, de Kanter, & Kugler, 2000). But it was not until the Mott Foundation, in partnership with the DOE, hosted a meeting on intentional learning in the winter of 2002 that there came to be a concerted focus on content and its delivery in afterschool programs.

Fortunately, while it is the beginning of the inquiry, it is not the end. All of these groups are committed to wrestling with the delivery of content in afterschool programs that link to the regular school day.

There are four main recommendations that come out of the chapter on bridging. First, make true two-way communication a priority. Second, integrate afterschool personnel into the life of the regular school day. Third, integrate youth development philosophy into teaching. Fourth, reexamine the restructuring of children's time.

School and afterschool personnel should be in regular communication with one another, especially on how best to bolster students' academic achievement. However, afterschool providers also need to be mindful that schools have confidentiality requirements around children's performance data. Therefore, schools and afterschool providers must develop strategies for how to break through these communication barriers.

Afterschool personnel need to be a vital part of the life of the school during the regular school day. It is already happening through vehicles like AmeriCorps and in programs like the 21st Century Community Learning Centers. One good way to make this happen is by hiring a full-time afterschool coordinator. Another is through training, training, and more training of volunteers, afterschool providers, and teachers.

Youth development may often be considered its own field, but youth development is also a philosophy that can be infused into education, as this books demonstrates. Training of school personnel is critical here. One good way that it can naturally occur is by employing teachers in afterschool programs who can bridge afterschool experiences with the school day and bring innovative techniques back into the regular classroom. These "bridging" teachers would be excellent peer mentors for their colleagues, especially since teachers learn best and prefer to learn from one another.

Finally, the fifth type of bridging (unified) that Noam and colleagues added to their bridging intensity typology since the Afterschool Settings: Learning with Excitement conference last spring should be rigorously studied because it adjusts the time of the core school day to accommodate both core academic subjects and supplemental activities. Thus, a core school day would no longer be thought of as an academic block from 8 A.M. to 3 P.M., but would be extended until 6 P.M., with supplemental or afterschool activities scheduled within that core time. Such a framework is not a new concept. In the United States, the community schools movement sought to keep the school building open to provide academic, enrichment, and recreational activities for students and adults alike. The community school programs, however, were driven by the desire to unify the community around a central institution, rather than to focus attention on improving children's academic performance. The model considered here is similar to that of our most elite private schools, as well as schools in Europe and Asia where supplemental activities are incorporated into the core day.

This model of extra learning time, as noted before, has been previously addressed within the context of public education, most notably in the report *Prisoners of Time*. The report argues that while there are many challenges in implementing a longer school day, a repackaged core day can relieve boredom, assist teachers in becoming a community of learners, and give kids more time to learn. All of these qualities have proven track records of effectiveness and could be of significant benefit to children in our poorest schools (de Kanter, Huff, & Chung, 2002).

References

Chung, A. M., de Kanter, A., & Kugler, M. (2000). Measuring and evaluating child and program outcomes in afterschool programs. *School-Age Review, 1*, 26–32.

de Kanter, A. L., Fiester, L., Lauland, A., & Romney, V. (1997). *Keeping schools open as community learning centers: Extending learning in a safe, drug-free environment before and after school.* Washington, DC: U.S. Department of Education.

de Kanter, A., Huff, M., & Chung, A. M. (2002, May). *Supplementation vs. supplantation: What is the core of schooling and what is supplemental?* Paper presented at the After-School Programs and Supplementary Education Conference, New York.

McLaughlin, M. (2000). *Community counts: How youth organizations matter for youth development.* Washington, DC: Public Education Network.

National Education Commission on Time and Learning. (1994). *Prisoners of time.* Washington, DC: U.S. Department of Education.

Policy Studies Associates. (1993). *The other 91 percent.* Washington, DC: Policy Studies Associates.

Seppanen, P. S., Love, J., deVries, D., Bernstein, L., Seligson, M., Marx, F., & Kisker, E. (1993). *National study of before- and after-school programs*. Washington, DC: U.S. Department of Education.

U.S. Department of Education. (1999). *Bringing education to the afterschool hours*. Washington, DC: U.S. Department of Education.

U.S. Department of Justice & U.S. Department of Education. (1998). *Safe and smart: Making after-school hours work for kids*. Washington, DC: Authors.

U.S. Department of Justice & U.S. Department of Education. (2000). *Working for children and families: Safe and smart afterschool programs*. Washington, DC: Authors.

Bridging Schools and Afterschool Programs

Sam Piha

Community Network for Youth Development

The reasons for schools and afterschool programs to work together in a more coordinated fashion are both clear and compelling. We know that children are best served when the adults who are most influential in their lives communicate and work together to support their growth and progress. We know that the most reliable predictor of a young person's success in early adulthood is school achievement, and that many young people lack the skills and supports to succeed. Finally, because many afterschool programs are required to operate on school sites and to provide young people with educational programming, we know that they will be most effective if they are working in concert with schoolday programs.

The authors of *Afterschool Education: Approaches to an Emerging Field* acknowledge that there are significant challenges to bridging school and afterschool settings. This is due in part to the tension that often exists between schools and the afterschool providers over the appropriate focus of afterschool programs. As we consider strategies to strengthen the partnerships between schools and afterschool programs, it is important to consider some of the fundamental issues that hold these parties apart.

One of the issues that contributes most heavily to this separation is that many afterschool programs are expected to improve students' performance in school. The measures of student performance, including grades and test scores, are the same measures used to judge schools themselves. Placing the burden of producing improved academic performance on afterschool programs has disenfranchised community providers who favor a more balanced and comprehensive approach to promoting young people's growth and development. In many communities it has pitted schools and providers against one another, and at times it has moved afterschool programs away from their strengths, resulting in their mimicking school-day practices in exchange for their share of the afterschool resources.

To those who have campaigned for increased access to afterschool programs, it appears that we have won the battle for the public's support and are now seeing an unprecedented level of financial allocation. However, it also appears that we have unwittingly accomplished this by continuing a tradition of formulating youth policy on a deficit model—one that defines young people as problems to be solved and youth programs as the problem-busters. We can now place academic failure at the top of a long list of problems that have defined youth policy and programming, from drug and alcohol use to early teen pregnancy, gang involvement, and juvenile crime.

Most would agree that afterschool programs can and should promote learning experiences and a variety of skills that contribute to young people's success in school. The question is how we can reframe the dialogue about learning in the afterschool hours in ways that bring together those who work with children in different settings around a shared vision. This vision must address what young people need to learn in order to succeed in school and in life, and where and when these things are best learned. Further, it must distinguish between the specific and unique contributions that schools and afterschool programs can offer. Addressing these questions would satisfy the challenge to build a bridge between school and afterschool that preserves and protects their distinct and differing strengths. This is not to suggest that afterschool programs should just go on "doing what they already do." In order to provide the high-quality support and opportunities that young people need in the out-of-school hours, afterschool programs should strive to create and establish quality measures to guide program design and improvement.

If we can broaden our definition of learning and assign appropriate accountability measures for afterschool programs, we can use this as a foundation for building stronger bridges between schools and afterschools. The first chapter of *Afterschool Education* offers an exciting typology of afterschool programs that helps us locate programs along a continuum of partnership with schools. It also offers recommendations, from the cataloging of best practices and the training of school and afterschool leaders to increased funding to support "staff bridges" that span the boundaries between school and afterschool.

We will only succeed by working at the local level. Many afterschool practitioners are working hard to win credibility and forge agreements with their host schools one principal at a time, one teacher at a time. The problem we are seeing, however, is that individuals within these settings are turning over at an alarming rate. Turnover in leadership and site-level staff can easily erode hard-fought gains.

What is sorely needed is leadership from those at the systems level—afterschool leaders and influential organizations and institutions that have the power to convene and influence others—to reopen the dialogue of learning in the afterschool hours, thereby offering schools and afterschool workers a clearer vision of how they each contribute to young people's learning needs. The goals of this work would include:

Drawing on the most up-to-date research about promoting learning in young people, especially in less formal learning environments. We need research-based knowledge about the kinds of things young people must learn in order to be productive both in and out of school, to connect positively with adults and peers, and to navigate their environments safely and successfully. There are two new studies that would be particularly useful: one, the Helping Communities Promote Youth Development Project by the National Academy of Sciences, and another by researchers James Connell and Michele Gambone of the Community Action for Youth Project (a joint project of Gambone and Associates and the Institute for Research and Reform in Education). Both study critical factors that promote healthy development across various settings. These factors include opportunities for learning that are designed to engage and challenge young people, program involvement that participants find meaningful and that promotes a sense of belonging, and the support of caring relationships with peers and adults. Also useful would be the long-term evaluation studies of existing afterschool programs, such as the soon-to-be-released evaluation of both the New York and San Francisco Beacon Centers. Both should yield important data about the relationship between the developmental experiences youth have within the programs and youth outcomes, including school success.

Creating a common language and framework for learning that schools and afterschool programs can agree on. Since educators and youth development advocates each carry their own frameworks and jargon, a focus on learning and the nature of effective learning environments represents common ground that both can endorse

Establishing appropriate measurements of outcomes and program quality that can guide program design and improvement. The measurements should be logically linked and scaled to actual program resources and offerings. For instance, standardized test scores are not appropriate outcomes of afterschool homework assistance programs; rather, these programs should be measured on outcomes related to what they can logically produce. Examples might include an increased rate of homework completion, improved homework grades, improved organizational skills, or greater self-reliance in completing homework.

Building on the strengths and accomplishments of the afterschool movement in order to preserve the appeal that afterschool holds for the public and for policymakers. Many programs have successfully offered effective educational support and enrichment for young people at risk of academic failure, an intended benefit that accounts for much of the support for afterschool programming. In determining how this benefit can be achieved more broadly, we need to consider the participants' range of needs and determine which roles are most appropriate for educators and for afterschool workers. We must also make the case that youth need to learn essential life skills, such as the ability to work effectively with others and assume responsibility, and higher-level thinking skills if they are to be successful in reaching their immediate and longer-term goals.

Implementing a strategy to disseminate a comprehensive depiction of what afterschool programs can accomplish, and educating and engaging policymakers and influential players at the national, state, and local levels. This is key, since the expectations for what afterschool programs can accomplish and how they should look must be championed by those who can wield influence among local systems and educational leaders.

If these efforts are led by an alliance of leaders in higher education (such as Harvard's Program in Afterschool Education and Research), afterschool programming, and youth development, we will gain greater clarity and unity among stakeholders in the field. When educators and youth development proponents at the systems and local levels come together to build bridges between school and afterschool, young people will experience more meaningful supports and opportunities and, in turn, will achieve greater success.

Supporting Children's Homework Assignments in Afterschool Programs

Harris Cooper

University of Missouri–Columbia

Homework can have many benefits for children that go beyond its immediate effects on achievement. It can help them develop good study habits so that they are ready to grow as their cognitive capacities mature. It can help children recognize that learning can occur outside as well as inside school. Homework can foster independent learning and responsible character traits. Homework can give parents and other adults an opportunity to see what is occurring in school and to express positive attitudes toward achievement.

But homework can also have negative effects. It can lead to boredom with schoolwork, since all activities remain interesting only for so long. Homework can deny children access to leisure activities that also teach important life skills. Parents and other adults can get too involved in homework. They can confuse children by using different instructional techniques than the teacher or by giving help that goes beyond tutoring.

Afterschool Education contains many innovative ideas about how best to fit homework into afterschool programs. The second chapter, "Extended Learning: School Content through Homework Support," directly discusses homework's place in afterschool programs, and points made in the chapter's recommendations raise some important issues.

Dedicated space. One recommendation in the chapter suggests that space in afterschool program settings should be dedicated to the completion of homework. However, while the recommendation is titled "Dedicated Space," the actual recommendation addresses personalized space. These are two different issues that need to be examined separately. It can be very important for children to personalize a space, but it is not necessarily the case that children must have a separate place to do their homework. For young children, a dedicated space may facilitate the completion of home-work but, similar to the circumstance for many families, if an afterschool program has limited space, it seems reasonable for space to be used for multiple purposes. This is not likely to have negative implications for the child or the quality of their homework, unless, of course, ambient noise and distractions are present. At home, many children recognize that they eat at the kitchen table, but then, at a certain time, the kitchen table is transformed into a homework space.

Time. The time recommendations are consistent with what research suggests is best homework practice. Specifically, all students should be as-signed homework (Cooper, 2001). However, the amount and type of homework they do should depend on their developmental level and the quality of their support at home. The National Parent Teacher Association and the National Education Association have a parent guide that states, "Most educators agree that for children in grades K–2, homework is most effective when it does not exceed 10–20 minutes each day; older children, in grades 3–6, can handle 30–60 minutes a day" (Henderson, 1996). Edu-cators often refer to this as "the ten-minute rule," or ten minutes multiplied by the student's grade level per night. These recommendations are consis-tent with the conclusions reached in my combined analyses of dozens of studies. If educators and parents expect homework far out of line with these recommendations to result in big gains in test scores, they are likely to be disappointed.

Internet resources. The chapter suggests that afterschool programs should seek out Internet help options. While this may be appropriate if computer access is readily available at a program site, general access to and facility with computers is still very closely tied to economic resources. Thus, as the authors of this book assert, the fact that public libraries may provide Internet service does not mean that teachers should feel comfortable as-signing homework that relies on computer access for successful comple-tion. Middle-class children will have computer access and skills that poor children do not.

The issue of computer access raises the more general point that home-work is not the great equalizer. Homework can accentuate existing social inequities. Children from poorer homes will have more difficulty completing assignments than their middle-class counterparts. Poorer children are less likely to have a quiet, well-lit place to do their assignments. Providing appropriate space and resources is one important support for homework that afterschool programs can supply.

Training and attitudes. In many ways, it seems that afterschool program staff can play much the same role as parents in the homework process. Therefore, the advice I often give to parents regarding how best to be involved in homework also seems appropriate to share with afterschool staff. Essentially, I offer five suggestions:

1. *Be a stage manager.* Program staff should make certain students in their program have a quiet, well-lit place to do homework. They should make sure the needed materials (such as paper, pencils, and dictionaries) are available.
2. *Be a motivator.* Homework provides a great opportunity for program staff to tell students how important school is. Staff should be positive about homework. The attitude expressed by adults about homework will affect the attitude developed by students in the program.
3. *Be a role model.* When students in an afterschool program are engaged in homework, staff should try to be involved in activities that mirror the homework activity. This will help the students see that the skills they are practicing are related to things they will do as adults.
4. *Be a monitor.* Program staff should watch students doing homework for signs of failure and frustration. If children ask for help, staff should provide guidance, not answers. If frustration sets in, staff should suggest a short break.
5. *Be a mentor.* When the teacher asks that an adult play a role in homework, program staff should do so willingly. If homework is meant to be done alone, staff should stay away. Homework is a great way for kids to develop independent, lifelong learning skills. Overinvolvement by adults can replace this fostering of independence with the notion that when things get difficult, an adult will do the work for them.

In sum, homework can have both positive and negative effects on students. As educators, parents, and concerned community members, it is our obligation to maximize the benefits and minimize the costs. Afterschool programs can play a critical role in achieving this goal.

References

Cooper, H. (2001). *The battle over homework: Common ground for administrators, teachers, and parents* (2nd ed.). Thousand Oaks, CA: Corwin Press.

Henderson, M. (1996). *Helping your student get the most out of homework.* Chicago: National Parent Teacher Association and the National Education Association. Retrieved November 2, 2000, from www.pta.org/Programs/edulibr/home work.htm

Affirming Culture and Building Citizenship through Afterschool Curricula

Maria del Pilar O'Cadiz

Collaborative After School Project, University of California, Irvine

Noam, Biancarosa, and Dechausay provide the burgeoning field of after-school education with a much-needed point of departure, developing a set of shared notions regarding existing curricular practices in afterschool settings. Their discussion in chapter three of afterschool curricular options and challenges serves as a reference point from which both researchers and practitioners can begin to reflect seriously on existing practices and develop innovative afterschool curricular approaches that avoid simple replication of in-school curriculum models, which historically have failed the very students we seek to reach (Beyer & Apple, 1998).

The Collaborative After School Project at the University of California, Irvine (UCI-CASP) shares with PAER an ongoing research interest in the nature of curriculum in afterschool programs and its related outcomes. UCI-CASP is committed to working with afterschool programss—specifically through training and resource development—to create learning experiences that are both engaging and beneficial to children and youth.[1] To this end, the California Department of Education has contracted with UCI-CASP to develop a series of curriculum guides, including a *New After-School and School-Age Care Curriculum Framework for the Elementary and Middle School Grades*, with accompanying guides offering specific activities in all subject areas. The guides will make explicit the connection between the afterschool activities and the state content standards for each subject area. The individual guides will describe best practices and offer sample activities

---

1. UCI-CASP currently works in partnership with the Los Angeles County Office of Education to provide technical assistance and training to all afterschool programs in the county.

that are aligned with the constructivist pedagogical principles and interdisciplinary approach outlined in the *Curriculum Framework*.

While PAER distinguishes between three kinds of learning that might take place in afterschool settings—extended, enriched, and intentional learning—the *Curriculum Framework* refers to afterschool curricula as "expanded learning opportunities" that do not "extend" the school day but expand on concepts and skills through well-organized and supervised activities (Collaborative After School Project [CASP], 2002, p. 8). Hence the concept of "expanded learning" matches PAER's category of "enriched learning." The *Framework* further defines it as "project-based learning activities" that may or may not be aligned with the typical academic subject matter students are expected to acquire in school. Additionally, the *Curriculum Framework* refers to "disguised learning," a term often used in the field to describe the broad range of activities that ultimately work to build academic skills but are distinguished by the informal, creative, and supportive environment in which they are carried out in afterschool program settings. Along these lines, the *Curriculum Framework* identifies three key components that distinguish afterschool curricula from academic activities that traditionally occur in classroom settings. Such afterschool curricula are:

1. child/youth centered, designed to meet the interests of children and youth;
2. open-ended, with flexible goals;
3. built around goals and objectives that go beyond specific academic skill-building to address social-emotional, health-related, and life skills.

Afterschool programmers also should organize their curricula thematically and allow for hands-on, active participation in integrated learning projects so that ideas and concepts are explored across a variety of disciplines, and so that children work together over time (CASP, 2002).

Whichever term is used—*expanded, enriched,* or *disguised learning*—the question remains as to *why* we want the learning experiences of children after school to be distinct from their in-school experiences. The common-sense answer is that children need to have fun after school. Indeed, afterschool programs should necessarily take the fun factor into account. From a child-development perspective, we need to recognize fully the value of play and peer interaction in the afterschool hours as a natural means of learning, and to think creatively about how to structure afterschool activities to optimize such natural learning opportunities.

For some educators, parents, and youth, the answer also lies in less lighthearted and more disheartening reality: namely, the persistent reality that the school curriculum all too often falls short of making meaningful connections to the daily lives, cultures, and community interests of students and their families, despite two decades of multicultural curriculum reform efforts in the schools. Hence, from the perspective of critical pedagogy,[2] cultural and community relevance are necessarily optimal characteristics for afterschool learning. Programs should work to distinguish afterschool learning experiences from what typically occurs in classrooms, which is dominated by mainstream culture and standards-based curriculum. Such a curricular approach would take the daily reality and cultural background of students and the sociohistorical experiences of the community as the basis for the themes and activities around which learning is organized. Curricular goals would go beyond (without ignoring) individual child development to address issues of the larger community context in which the children participating in the program live. Because afterschool programs generally have the opportunity to build direct connections with families and community members, these programs are an ideal setting for addressing the complex realities outside the school walls through culturally meaningful and community-oriented learning.

In my work as an afterschool program director in Boyle Heights (a Latino immigrant community east of Los Angeles), I had the opportunity to design and implement a curriculum that began with an investigation of the pre-Columbian history of the students' ancestors. The third-, fourth-, and fifth-grade students read Aztec mythological stories, made clay figurines of

2. According to Sonia Nieto (1992), "Critical pedagogy is not simply the transfer of knowledge from teacher to students . . . [rather, from a critical multicultural paradigm,] it reflects on multiple and contradictory perspectives to understand reality more fully. Critical pedagogy is based on the experiences and view points of students rather that on an imposed culture" (pp. 220–221).

pre-Columbian artifacts, and collectively drew out time lines of the different civilizations that existed in the very places from which their parents immigrated only a few years before. They drew maps outlining the journeys that their families took to get to Los Angeles; measured distances; interviewed parents, grandparents, aunts, and uncles; and wrote their families' oral histories. They painted murals representing what they had learned about their families' histories and cultural beliefs, all the while building a stronger sense of self and community membership. I recently attended the year-end event of the same afterschool program, which is now called the Boyle Heights College Institute. Two students who had participated in the early days of the program proudly announced their high school graduation and entrance into the University of California and California State University. The program curriculum—through its authentic connection to the realities and experiences of the families it served—had supported these students in their academic success.

In a distinctive effort to support the proliferation of such culturally relevant curricula in afterschool programs, the Oakland-based nonprofit organization California Tomorrow is currently conducting a national research project called the Access and Equity in After School Programs Project. Funded by the Mott Foundation, the study's purpose is "to increase attention and dialogue, and to contribute to the knowledge base about effective policies and practices in the after school field related to improving access to after school programs and improving educational and social outcomes for low-income and minority youth and communities" (California Tomorrow, 2002). This project looks at how programs address diversity in their curricula and make efforts to connect explicitly with the culture of the children, parents, and community. It involves both qualitative case studies of diverse program sites and a national survey.[3] One of the promising practice sites selected by the California Tomorrow researchers, California Living Histories (CLH),[4] uses the visual arts to build the literacy skills and academic confi-

3. Research staff at UCI-CASP, including O'Cadiz, have participated in the design of the national survey, "Quality After School Services in the Context of Diversity."

4. CLH is a community-based educational project that has been providing afterschool programming primarily to Latino and African American students at elementary schools in the Pasadena Unified School District since 1999.

dence of students. The CLH program also engages traditionally disenfranchised parents in the education of their children while exploring issues of identity, community, and culture. The CLH curriculum is organized as a series of eight-week thematic projects, led by experienced community artists and educators, in which students are invited to recognize who they are and to imagine themselves as part of a diverse and vibrant community. Activities include self-portraits, identity T-shirts, prose and poetry, family oral histories, videography, community murals and gardens, and end-of-year art exhibits. Immigrant parents have expressed the importance of the CLH programming in validating their cultural heritage and their family's contribution to their new land.

As evidenced in these two programs, the afterschool field presents a set of possibilities for the effort to carry out progressive educational work with traditionally underserved or poorly served populations. Specifically, afterschool offers an opportunity to bring together multiple spheres of action into mutually supportive networks of people and resources. This allows for a different kind of curriculum: one in which we can work collaboratively— alongside students, parents, community educators and volunteers, and committed professionals—to create programs that respond more directly to students' identities and interests.

To provide these kinds of distinctive learning opportunities, afterschool program staff need to understand the community in which a program operates and the children and youth with whom they work. They also need the capacity (i.e., technical skills) and opportunity (through democratic program management models) to bring that knowledge base into their program's curriculum design. This is in line with the PAER authors' recommendation that afterschool programs train staff in the use of project-based curriculum. Programs would also be enhanced if staff were encouraged to be creative in the curriculum design process and to develop projects that were culturally appropriate and socially significant to the specific populations they serve.

In sum, afterschool program settings should allow children and youth to engage in learning activities that are distinctively constructivist in their pedagogical approach and, where possible, involve social action or some form of service learning. Afterschool curriculum themes should be derived not from the staid content of traditional school curricula but should stem from the daily lives of the students, their cultural backgrounds, and their community histories. Activities should also invite students to explore and understand their community's contemporary situation. This is not to refuse to link afterschool learning to school academic objectives or to further disenfranchise communities by divesting them of the cultural capital necessary for their effective navigation of the broader society. Rather, it is a recognition of our duty as educators (whether we work in school or afterschool) to ensure that all students have equitable access and that such access can be based on the immense knowledge resources that reside in their communities. Afterschool curricula based on the more complex project-based learning that Noam, Biancarosa, and Dechausay describe in this book, as well as the meaningful involvement of parents and other community members, can thus serve to create experiences that enrich school learning, help students make connections between academic content and their daily lives, promote positive self-identity, and support the development of an active citizenry.

References

Beyer, L. E., & Apple, M. W. (1998). *The curriculum: Problems, politics and possibilities.* Albany: State University of New York Press.

California Tomorrow. (2002). *Promising practices in after school equity/diversity.* Oakland, CA: Author.

Collaborative After School Project (CASP). (2002). *New after-school/school-age program curriculum framework for the elementary and middle school grades.* Irvine: University of California.

Nieto, S. (1992). *Affirming diversity: The sociopolitical context of multicultural education.* New York: Longman.

About the Contributors

Gil G. Noam is a clinical and developmental psychologist. He is Director of the Program in Afterschool Education and Research at the Harvard Graduate School of Education and of the Laboratory of Developmental Psychology at McLean Hospital/Harvard Medical School. He is the founder of the RALLY (Responsive Advocacy for Life and Learning in Youth) Prevention Programs in Boston, which are located in schools and in afterschool settings.

Gina Biancarosa is an advanced doctoral student in Language and Literacy at the Harvard Graduate School of Education and a Research Assistant at the Program in Afterschool Education and Research. She has served as a member of the teaching team of The Afterschool Child: Development, Programming, and Policy, a graduate course at Harvard. A Spencer Research Training Grant recipient, her research interests include afterschool education, reading comprehension, and theory of mind.

Nadine Dechausay has served as a Research Assistant and Community Liaison at the Program in Afterschool Education and Research. She has coordinated the placement of Harvard Graduate School of Education students in afterschool programs across Boston and Cambridge. She has also been part of the development and teaching team of the Harvard graduate course, The Afterschool Child: Development, Programming, and Policy. She is currently enrolled in the M.A. program at the Ontario Institute for Studies in Education of the University of Toronto.

Marcelo M. Suárez-Orozco is the Victor S. Thomas Professor of Education at the Harvard Graduate School of Education, codirector of the Harvard Immigration Project, and chair of the Interfaculty Committee on Latino Studies at Harvard University. Suárez-Orozco's work is in the areas of cultural psychology and psychological anthropology, with a focus on the study of immigration.

Reed Larson is a Professor in the Departments of Human and Community Development, Psychology, and Educational Psychology at the University of Illinois at Urbana-Champaign. His research focuses on the daily experience of adolescents and their parents.

Adriana de Kanter serves as Partnership Liaison in the Office of Elementary and Secondary Education of the U.S. Department of Education. She is the author of numerous books and articles on education issues affecting children in afterschool programs, family involvement in children's learning, limited English-proficient populations, children at risk of academic failure, and proper nutrition.

Sam Piha is Director for Community and School Partnerships for the Community Network for Youth Development. He has been involved in the fields of youth development, adolescent counseling, and childhood education since 1975.

Harris Cooper is a Professor in the Department of Psychological Sciences at the University of Missouri–Columbia. He has conducted extensive research on homework and is currently updating his synthesis of research on the topic.

Maria del Pilar O'Cadiz is Executive Director of the Collaborative After School Project (CASP) at the University of California, Irvine. CASP is a research and technical assistance project that develops afterschool curriculum and program management resources for the California Department of Education. She also services afterschool programs in Los Angeles County through trainings and on-site mentoring.